PRAISE FOR
ECHOES OF A GLOBAL LIFE

"Echoes of a Global Life" is a fascinating first-person account of a unique ex-pat upbringing in a time and in a world that no longer exists. Part memoir, part travel log, part history, Kathleen Gamble shares her adventures and observations as a third culture kid, raised by parents in foreign lands, drawn to living internationally herself, and finally as mother to a son who is also a global nomad. I highly recommend "Echoes of a Global Life".

–Professor Tina Norton Buck, Austin, Texas

"By turns entertaining and disturbing, hopeful and heartbreaking, Kathleen Gamble's story is a window into a world most people never experience—where letting go is a way of life, and roots never have time to take hold. Where resilience means reinventing oneself for each new place and time. A magnificent portrait of the timeless search for home."

–A.A.Vogel, author of *Call of the Desert: Crossing* (Beloved Daughter series)

"Kathleen Gamble's *Echoes of a Global Life* is an unflinchingly honest account of her experiences as a Third Culture Kid (TCK) or Global Nomad as those of us who have grown-up across the globe call ourselves. "Rootless" and "Restless" is how she describes herself after a life living on several continents, several of which affected her profoundly during her formative years. Despite our best intentions we never quite fit in, but we bring an extraordinary cross-cultural adaptability and resilience that benefits our communities and careers which Ms. Gamble describes eloquently."

–Diana B. Putman, Ph.D., Retired USAID Senior Foreign Service Officer

"Life as a global nomad sounds enticing, unless you're a child who has no say in it. Kathleen Gamble grew up in Burma, Latin America, Nigeria, and in boarding schools. Those experiences enriched her but left her feeling adrift. She followed her husband to Moscow in the chaotic

1990s, an adventure that ended badly. Now on her own in the U.S., she has written this book to make sense of the grief and the bond she shares with other Third Culture Kids.

–Carol Matlack, Former Foreign Correspondent, living in Paris

"In 1961, Kathleen Gamble's mother broke her ankle jumping off the wing of a crashed and burning airplane. Her father held Kathy in his arms when he jumped, she was five years old. They were both unhurt. Her two older brothers jumped, too, and walked away. Seventeen people died in the crash. And so begins Kathleen Gamble's delightful engrossing, courageous and painfully honest tale of growing up as a TCK (Third Culture Kid) and the fascinating life that followed.

"Kathleen was born in Burma and went to elementary and high schools in Mexico, Columbia, Nigeria, Switzerland and the United States with dozens of detailed anecdotes including journal entries and excerpts from letters written with the color, words and urgency of the time describing the life of a kid forever adapting.

"*Growing up I always felt like an object. In Latin America, I figured it was the culture that made the men prey on me and harass me. But when I moved to Africa, the men were the same. They were the same the world over.*" There is feminist quality to the book, an insistence on her woman-ness within the routine misogyny she confronts across the world. Her feminism is not an intellectualism or a cudgel, but is rather the dispassionate recounting of the assumptions and bigotries of the cultures around her exacerbated by environment, language and the isolation of the boarding schools she attended. In high school, she was raped by a friend and classmate, an incident she describes with a candor and precision that reveals the horror of the moment.

"*Echoes of a Global Life* is a unique and fascinating portrait of a woman striding the world to her own fife; to this day, she flies regularly and hates it."

–Stephen Banks, writer at *Americaisabeautifulthing.com*

ECHOES OF A
GLOBAL LIFE

Wisdom
Editions

Minneapolis

FIRST EDITION AUGUST 2025
Echoes of a Global Life. Copyright © 2025 by Kathleen Pilugin.
All rights reserved.

No part of this book may be used or reproduced in any manner whatsoever without written permission except in the case of brief quotations used in critical articles and reviews.

For information, write to Calumet Editions,
6800 France Avenue South, Suite 370, Edina, MN 55435

10 9 8 7 6 5 4 3 2 1
ISBN: 978-1-962834-53-7

Cover and interior design: Gary Lindberg

ECHOES OF A GLOBAL LIFE

KATHLEEN GAMBLE

Minneapolis

Thank you to Bill and Virginia, my parents, for introducing me to a life full of learning and adventure.

CONTENTS

PREFACE 1
July 1961 5
PART ONE 11
    Rangoon 1952-1954 13
    Pyinmata 1954-1959 17
    Rangoon 1961 21
    The Exit 27
    Rye, New York 31
PART TWO 33
    Mexico City 1963 35
    Las Lomas 41
    Snapshots from Mexico 45
    Guatemala and El Salvador 1968 51
    Austin 1969 53
    The Beach 1971 61
    Colegio Nueva Granada 65
    El Lago 69
    On to Africa 75
PART THREE 77
    Lagos, Nigeria 1972 79
    Back to Boarding School, Lugano, Switzerland 89
    Snapshots from Europe 97
    California 1974 101
    On Safari in Kenya and Tanzania 105
    Ibadan, Nigeria 111
    Snapshots from Nigeria 115
    Boston 1976 123
    Winding Up My African Experience 127
PART FOUR 133
    Denver 1978 135
    Minneapolis 1980 139

Marriage	145
Washngton, DC	149
Moscow	151

PART FIVE. **155**

Arrival 1993	157
Learning to Buy Bread	161
Getting Around Moscow	167
The British Embassy	171
Political Unrest	175
Typical Moscow Life	181
Apartment Two	183
Snapshots from Russia	185
Apartment Three	191
Apartment Four	193
Apartment Five	199
American Women	203
Total Eclipse of the Sun	207
Apartment Six	209
Back to Lugano	213
New Tear's Resolution	217
A Quick Exit	219

PART SIX. **225**

The Aftermath 2001	227
Another New Place	231
Moving On	235
My Last Move?	239

AFTERWORD: THE TRAVELS CONTINUE. **243**

ABOUT THE AUTHOR **257**

"If you reject the food, ignore the customs, fear the religion and avoid the people, you might better stay at home."

–James Michener

PREFACE

Like all lives, mine has been a journey—sometimes an exciting one, sometimes traumatic, sometimes happy, but always a little sad. Challenging, uneasy, confusing, but rarely boring. My key words are *rootless* and *restless*. Everything is temporary; change is constant. When I meet a person for the first time, I tell them my name. I hear their name, then immediately forget it. I cannot retain a name after only one meeting. To be honest, I do not even listen. Once I get to know them a little and have something to associate them with, then I ask them their name again. Then it usually sticks. Because I've moved over thirty times and said goodbye to hundreds of people, retaining a name based on one or two meetings seems impossible. Immediately after hearing and forgetting their name, I am asked, "And where are you from?"

This question makes my mind go blank.

"Uhhh…"

What do I say? Do I make something up? Do I tell the truth? Do I pretend to ignore it?

In the meantime, I hear, "It's not that difficult of a question." Or: "The questions get harder from here."

I laugh. "I live in Minnesota." This works best if I am not actually in Minnesota.

Or: "My family comes from Iowa." I usually do not get a lot of follow up questions from that one unless the person is from Iowa. Or: "I moved around a lot." Keep it vague.

If you choose to make up a place, it helps to have been there. My brother used to tell people he was from Omaha because he was born there, but he had never really been. Every once in a while, he would run into somebody who *was* from there and he would be in trouble. "What high school did you go to? What neighborhood did you live in?" Obviously, he had no answer.

The truth is, I do not know where I am from. The US is my passport country and always has been. But I have never felt at home in my passport country. I was born in Burma (now called Myanmar). I grew up in Mexico, Colombia, Nigeria, Switzerland, and the US. I went to three different high schools. I am from everywhere and nowhere.

When I arrived in the US to go to college after living most of my life in other countries, I faced problems. I looked and talked like an American, but I was not like my fellow Americans. I did not know anything about American pop culture, TV, or history. I was more like the foreign students than the Americans. Much later in life I discovered there were other people like me who had trouble adjusting to their passport country, people like me who had lived all over the world because of their parents' work. We did not choose it or have a say in it—we just accepted it. The good and the bad.

Some call us global nomads, Third Culture Kids (TCKs), cultural chameleons, cultural hybrids, the misunderstood, or hidden immigrants. We're in our own special box. Ruth Useem, an American sociologist and anthropologist, first coined the term Third Culture Kid in the 1950s. It referred to children who spent their formative years in countries that were not their passport country. The first culture was the passport culture of their parents, the second was the country they lived in, and the third was the one they blended into and made their own. My third culture is a mix of about six cultures.

Of course there are other people who have had similar experiences. People who have lived in many different states in US also have trouble adapting and fitting in. Military kids are one example. They move around often and some go overseas. Immigrants, refugees, children of immigrants, and people who have parents from different cultures (or Cross Cultural Kids) can have similar challenges.

There are pros and cons of growing up the way I did. For the most part, TCKs are resilient, tolerant, and open minded. We accept cultural differences, are good negotiators, are well educated, speak different languages, and adjust to new situations quickly. We can, however, also have a confused sense of identity, tend to be restless and rootless, and can have difficulty developing relationships. And we have a lot of grief—usually unresolved grief. As children it is not always easy to process all the losses you experience when you are constantly saying goodbye to people and places, and it can carry over into adulthood.

I read one of my stories of my experience as a TCK for a group of people recently and afterwards they reacted to it by saying how scary it was. Yes, sometimes things could go either way and could be scary, but I pushed through it somehow. I do not usually get scared, but instead I go into survival mode and weigh my options. When I went to Egypt recently a woman asked my father if he was worried about me going to that part of the world. He said, "No, she can take care of herself."

So, my life has not been all butterflies and rainbows, but I have had lots of great experiences. Some were funny, some crazy. Some were sad, some good. Several are even unbelievable.

Where am I from? Where is home? It could be anywhere. Come along with me and find out.

JULY 1961

July 12, 1961, The Evening Sentinel, Shenandoah, Iowa

Keith Gamble Family Escape in Plane Crash

Keith Gamble, 41, and the four members of his family who survived the plane wreck at Denver Tuesday, are pondering their next move today. The Gambles were enroute to Rangoon, Burma, where he was to resume his duties as farm advisor with the Ford Foundation.

Dr. Gamble and his family had been visiting his parents, Mr. and Mrs. Frank Gamble and relatives here a week, leaving Shenandoah Tuesday morning for Burma, where they had previously spent seven years.

From a suite at the Hilton Hotel in Denver, Dr Gamble talked to his brother, Paul Gamble last night and said they had all been checked at a hospital and dismissed. Mrs. Gamble is on crutches with a broken arch in her foot but is with the family at the hotel. She was injured when she jumped from the wrecked plane. As he went out the door, Tom, 13, had his hair singed from an explosion. They were on the left side of the plane which was the first to burst into flames. Their seats, however, were near the front of the jet. Tim, 15, and Kathy, 4, escaped unhurt.

Dr Gamble will talk to the Ford Foundation today and

made plans accordingly. The Gambles were to leave Los Angeles Thursday by plane for the Philippines, where they planned to spend several days. The two boys are to enter a private school there in the fall. Tim and Tom expected to accompany their parents to Rangoon, then return to the Philippines. Dr Gamble was to report for duty July 23. The last two years have been spent in the United States, while he was studying for his doctor's degree at Cornell University, Ithaca, N.Y.

Start Investigation DC8 Which Crashed at Denver Killing 17; 105 Survive

By Frank Wetzel

Denver (AP)—Federal investigators rummaged through the torn skeleton of a United Air Lines DC8 jetliner today to learn the exact cause of Tuesday's crash landing and fire in which 17 persons died.

The huge plane en-route to Los Angeles from Philadelphia touched the runway, veered sideways and burst into flames.

Of the 122 aboard, 18 persons escaped injury in the holocaust. Fifty others went to Denver hospitals. The other 56 aboard, including the crew of 7, escaped serious injury.

A civil engineer, Henry Bloom, 52, driving a Surrey truck for the city, was killed when the big plane swerved off the runway and crushed the truck.

In addition to Bloom, 16 plane passengers died. They included five men, seven women and four children.

The plane on Flight 859 had made earlier stops in Chicago and Omaha.

Passengers said they were alerted by the pilot, Capt. John Grosso of Denver, 10 minutes before the crash that something was the matter with the hydraulics system, an important element in the brakes.

There was a strange mixture of quiet calm and anguished desperation when the plane touched the runway, then skidded off, crossed 100 yards of field and burst into huge billows of flame when the landing gear crumpled on the protruding strip of a concrete taxiway being constructed nearby.

Crackle, crackle, "Blah, blah, blah," crackle, "Blah, blah, blah, blah."

My four-year-old brain could not understand or process what the man was saying over the loudspeaker. I only sensed it was bad. People around me looked nervous. My father was sitting next to me on the aisle. I watched him take out his briefcase from under the seat, remove his glasses and put them in his pocket. I was not sure why. I wondered if I should retrieve my doll, Meredith, from under my seat. Would she be safe?

Bam! We hit the ground but did not bounce, just kept going as the plane swerved. I tried to hold on as the plane shook and tossed us around. Things were flying through the cabin, hats and bags sailing through the air. Then suddenly we came to an abrupt halt. Immediately my father picked me up and ran towards the back of the plane, my mother in front of us. My brothers Tom, thirteen, and Tim, fifteen, were behind us. We squeezed through a window exit and stepped out onto the wing. The engines were on fire, with flames coming up one whole side of the wing. My mother was down on the ground but could not walk. A man was helping her get up and across the runway from the grassy edge where the plane had stopped.

My father, however, froze on the wing. My brothers were no longer behind us. Other people were coming out but not them. Realizing this, my father did not budge. The heat from the fire was intense. Finally, they came through the window exit and my father jumped onto the ground and ran across the runway to my mother. He immediately went into severe shock. He was holding me so tightly that the shock passed to me, and I began screaming in terror. He would not let me go even though my mother pleaded with him to put me down.

The fire trucks could not get onto the runway due to construction of some kind. The necessary ramps were missing. We stood by the side of the runway watching the chaos for what seemed like hours. Somehow, we ended up in a large hangar where each passenger had to tell the airline authorities who they were and what luggage they had. Some were sent to a nearby hospital. A doctor tended to my mother since she broke her foot when she jumped from the wing onto the ground. She hobbled around on crutches. (Note to self: Remember to take your high heels off when jumping out of airplanes.) We were then sent off to a hotel in town. In the car my parents told us the airline would replace everything that was lost, and I had to ask if that included my toothbrush. I could have lived without that. I was particularly sad to lose my baby doll, Meredith, because she really could never be replaced, which I knew, even at four years old.

Seventeen people died in the crash and many more were severely burned. My father and brothers had minor burns, and my mother had a broken foot, and we were all traumatized. One of the reasons airlines now have the long safety speech at the beginning of flights is because of that day in Denver in 1961. The crew was not properly trained, and people did not know what to do in case of an emergency. Many died from smoke inhalation because they could not find their way out. My family and I were lucky.

Several days later, my father showed up at the hotel with one of our suitcases. It was the only one that was identifiable; all the others had burned up. We opened it and all we saw were ashes and partially burned items.

My mother, Virginia, never wrote about the plane crash directly. She referred to it many times in later years, mostly when things were lost, or she was moving. It taught her (and all of us) to not get attached to material things since that day everything had burned up. The crash did have a lasting effect on the family and manifested itself in different ways, but the reality was this was only the first leg of our journey halfway around the world.

> July 18, Denver Hilton, Colorado
>
> We are gradually getting squared around—have some shopping done, Bill had a physical (all ok) yesterday and the Dr also looked at my foot, we have our luggage (much of it still empty), we have consulted a lawyer (just to be sure we will be well represented in case any difficulty should arise—our friend in Rochester suggested this when Bill called him) and expect to leave for Los Angeles tomorrow.
>
> United called this afternoon and said they found 3 passports (the boys' and Bill's) two in good condition, also my Tri-Delt pin and Bill's fraternity pin!! Perhaps more jewelry will turn up.
>
> My foot is much better, I can walk without the crutches some but the doctor said I should keep them and use them a while longer though. I might use just one part of the time if I like. They are most uncomfortable to use, besides being cumbersome.
>
> We visited North Pole, Colorado yesterday on our way up Pike's Peak and Kathy visited with Santa and we got her a Tiny Tears baby doll plus clothes and bottle. The doll cries real tears and wets, so her clothes are always damp! Kathy calls her Judy Margaret and is real pleased with her.
>
> Love, Virginia

I have no recollection of that doll.

After shopping, we took a few days R & R in a cabin in Colorado Springs where we ran into a cousin of mine on the street. He knew all about the plane crash, of course. One bright spot of the whole ordeal was that I got the coolest cowgirl outfit ever. Dang, I was one crazy cowgirl!

From Denver we continued on to Los Angeles and Hawaii for a few days to visit relatives, then to the Philippines to investigate my brothers' new boarding school and finally landed in Rangoon, Burma on my fifth birthday—two weeks later than originally planned.

I found out years later that as a child every time we boarded a plane, I would become physically ill. I have no recollection of this. I asked my brother about it, but he must have blocked it out as well. My older brother himself had a delayed reaction and dreaded flying most of his adult life. My mother took anti-anxiety pills to tolerate the many flights she endured. My other brother and my father seemed to take it all in stride and never mentioned having any problems. Because of my family's lifestyle, most of the time I had no choice but to fly. There was a period of about six years when we lived in Mexico that I did not fly, but that was my only respite. To this day, I always have a stomachache in anticipation. But I love to travel, so I set my brain to autopilot and get on the plane anyway.

PART ONE

RANGOON 1952-1954

During the Second World War my father, William K. Gamble, flew blimps off the coast of Brazil for the US Navy. He had grown up on a farm in Iowa and as he traveled through the Brazilian countryside, he witnessed the poverty and saw farms that were not producing. These early experiences inspired him to get his master's degree in Agricultural Education so he could travel and work in other countries and hopefully make a difference. Nine years after my parents married, my father went to work for the Technical Cooperation Agency (TCA, a precursor to USAID). He was assigned to the Burmese State Teacher Training College where he worked with students in agriculture. My parents and my two brothers, who were four and six years old, started their great expat adventure in 1952. Their friends and relatives thought they had lost their minds. This was before jet airplanes, a polio vaccine, and long before the Internet.

As my mother, Virginia, drove through the streets of Calcutta on a stopover enroute to Burma in 1952, she saw real poverty for the first time. She had been naive about the world and had adjustment problems and culture shock. Despite this, she kept an open mind, stayed optimistic, and wanted to learn to understand her new surroundings.

After living in Rangoon for a while she sent a letter to her local newspaper back in Iowa.

I would like to tell you so much about Burma and our life here, but it is hard to condense all these new experiences and decide which might be the most interesting.

First, I think you might like to know what our home is like. We are fortunate in having a good-sized brick house which is rented from a Burmese woman. It has 20-ft ceilings, ceiling fans, concrete floors, and every piece of wood in the whole house from rafters to coffee table is beautiful teakwood! To help run our household we have a cook who is indispensable, for he does the marketing, acts as interpreter since he speaks excellent English as well as four or five other languages, and he miraculously runs the temperamental kerosene stove! Then we have a sweeper who does the cleaning which includes scrubbing the concrete floors and waxing all the furniture at least once a week to prevent mildew. Then, since babysitters are unheard of here as such, we have a nanny who lives with us and, besides babysitting, takes care of the light laundry, helps me with mending and sewing and is a most pleasant person to have around. She is young, pretty and a good Baptist. I usually take her with me when I drive so that she can interpret for me if the car should break down or if we should become lost.

Now as Mother keeps asking, you must be wondering what I do with my new "life of leisure." Well, everything is not perfect and leisurely even with so much help, believe me! Since many people in this part of the world do not have the same ideas of sanitation as we do, I have to constantly check on the kitchen to be sure the water is boiled before placed in the refrigerator for drinking, to remind the dishwasher to use soap, to see that clean dishtowels regularly replace dirty ones, etc. Our help is very fine, really, and they do everything to make us comfortable, but they often do not realize how particular we must be to avoid becoming sick. One day I found the nanny straining fresh boiled drinking water through a very dirty napkin into a pitcher! I am trying to learn to speak Burmese, I keep all the household accounts, of course, and do most of the meal planning, attend meetings of several organizations, read as much as possible, go out socially some, and write letters. It does not sound like much, I guess, but time is passing very quickly.

Rangoon is a most colorful and interesting city with large Chinese and Indian populations as well as the pleasant, friendly Burmese. The city is dominated by one very tall gold-roofed pagoda (the Shwe Dagon Pagoda) which is a most interesting place to visit besides being a landmark for Rangoon and one of the outstanding pagodas in this part of the world. One climbs hundreds of steps to the top where there are many statues of Buddha of different sizes, colors and positions. The roof or dome of the pagoda is pure gold-leaf, and it has many valuable gems sealed inside. We enjoyed the long climb to the top almost as much as the worship center, for the stairs are lined with little shops where everything one can imagine is sold - Burmese drums, ankle bracelets, cymbals, flowers, lacquerware, ivory combs, flutes made of bamboo, brassware, and toys. Once Bill and I wanted to buy a delightful-sounding Burmese gong, and since one bargains over the price of most everything we started bargaining. The merchant asked 15 rupees, we offered 6 and finally after much haggling got it for 8 rupees - very pleased with our bargain. When we got home, one of our servants pointed out a price mark written in Burmese - 5 rupees!! But we had had fun anyway, and you can be sure we learned how to read Burmese numbers that very day!

We really like it here in Rangoon and are so glad we had the opportunity to come. It is a joy to find that these people halfway around the world are just the same as Americans are, and that it is as easy to become good friends with Asians as it is with Iowans. This is one of the things that gives me a renewed faith in the world.

She had her ups and downs, but I think she and the rest of my family genuinely liked living in Burma. They lived there a total of seven years. I showed up after they moved to Pyinmana.

PYINMANA 1954-1959

In 1954, the Ford Foundation established an office in Rangoon. The Ford Foundation was funded by Henry Ford and his son Edsel, initially by a small amount in the 1930s and then fully funded by the early 1950s. It was completely separate from the Ford Motor Company with its own Board of Directors and headquarters in New York City. For a long time, it was by far the largest private charitable organization (though now the Gates and other foundations are larger). It still has assets of about ten billion dollars and its operating expenses and grants are about 500 million dollars a year. My father worked for the Ford Foundation for thirty years, two years at a time since they only hired people on two-year contracts. He worked in the US, Burma, Mexico, Central America, the Caribbean, Colombia, Venezuela, and West and Central Africa.

Since the TCA support was about to end, the Burmese Director of Education approached the Ford Foundation representative, Dr. John Everton, to see if they would be interested in supporting the development of the Pyinmana Agricultural Institute. In January 1955, my father went to work for the Ford Foundation and my family moved to Pyinmana, halfway between Rangoon and Mandalay on the road north.

That was when I came into the picture. In July 1956, my mother and my brothers went to live with friends in Rangoon. About a month later I was born at the Seventh Day Adventist Hospital. The doctor who delivered me was an American from Nebraska. Two telegrams went out from that hospital. One to my grandparents in the US and one to my father. My grandparents in Iowa, halfway around the world, got their telegram almost immediately. My father, who was up-country in Pyinmana, did not hear anything about me until two days later.

I spent the first three years of my life in Pyinmana speaking Hindi, Tamil, Karen, Burmese, and English. Our household help were from India and Burma, and I spoke to everybody in their own language. We lived upstairs in a huge old brick house on the campus of the Agricultural Institute. The downstairs had been used as a pig pen and when my parents moved in there was still a sow there about to have a litter of pigs. The refrigerator and stove ran on kerosene because the electricity came and went. We had indoor bathrooms but never hot water. At night we slept under mosquito nets. The house looked out over rice fields to a range of wooded mountains that provided us with cool breezes.

There were still insurgents in the area, and we would hear the occasional gunfight off in the distance. My brother delighted in this. "Are those *real* bullets?" he would ask excitedly.

Since we were on the campus of an agricultural school, my mother's letters also detailed the constant animal problems. One of the pigs died of anthrax. And some nights everybody was up worrying over the chicken eggs in the incubators. It took a while to get it right. Our pets were always getting injured or sick or giving birth. A stray dog bit my father and he had to have thirteen rabies shots.

And then there was human health. We had one Indian doctor in the area who was very good but with no telephone, reaching him could take some time. My mother relied heavily on Dr. Spock's book *The Common Sense Book of Baby and Child Care*, which was first published in 1946. Dysentery was common, I got the measles with high fever and convulsions, my brother got the mumps, my father got food poisoning, and our cook got smallpox. Of course, all these things drove my mother over the edge. Here she was in up-country Burma hours from the nearest hospital with one doctor with limited resources and small children to take care of. She did her best to make sure the water was boiled, the vegetables washed, the house clean, and she watched me closely to try to monitor what I put in my mouth. One thing I liked to do was pick up ants off the ground and eat them. That was something she remembered well. People in the open market were always trying to feed me. I think that upset her even more than the ants.

I always woke up before the rest of the family and my nanny would take me for a walk. Sometimes she would take me to the neighbor's house where they were also early risers, and Mrs. Hewitt would make me pancakes. I loved that. There was a small bridge by one of the school buildings and we would often stop there. I imagined all kinds of people living under it and I would play with these imaginary friends. In reality, I lived in a house full of people and neighbors were always dropping in. I was spoiled by all the attention since I was one of the youngest children in the compound. I do not remember a lot about those first years in Burma but whenever I smell curry, I think of my Indian nanny. I always think of dhal as comfort food and the smell of mildew reminds me of "home."

At the beginning of 1959, my father decided it was time to return to school for a doctorate degree. At three years old I said goodbye to everything I knew and the people I loved in Burma to move to Ithaca, New York. A strange new place. We moved into a three-bedroom house and at times I would find myself standing in a room alone. I would scream and scream in a panic until somebody found me and reassured me they were still nearby. This went on for a while as I had trouble adjusting to my new environment. I could not be separated from my family. I was confused. Why were people not familiar to me? What was this new place?

After two years I was beginning to settle in when once again, I had to say goodbye to my new friends and many of my belongings to get on an airplane and travel back halfway around the world. My father graduated from Cornell with a PhD in Education with minors in Agricultural Economics and Sociology. I graduated from nursery school and my brother, Tim, graduated from junior high. I remember I learned to sing "My Bonnie Lies over the Ocean" in nursery school. The big hit on the radio at the time was "Itsy Bitsy Teenie Weenie Yellow Polka Dot Bikini." I always envisioned Bonnie in that bikini floating over the ocean.

The Ford Foundation rehired my father and sent him back to Burma as a specialist in agriculture. And as I said, on our way back to Burma we all survived the plane crash.

RANGOON 1961

In 1961, I was enrolled in kindergarten at the International School in Rangoon where I had a Burmese teacher who wore beautiful longyis (a traditional wraparound skirt) and tied her hair up in a bun. She had taught my brothers and remembered them, so that made me feel a little more comfortable. I only went for half a day, so I was always home for lunch. Since it was an international school, there were kids from all over the world, but the language spoken was English.

One day I was at school and the alarm went off. The loud siren reverberated through the halls. Why was it so loud? What was going on? We filed out and stood away from the building, looking at it. Somebody mentioned fire. A fire drill. What was that? I cried and screamed in a panic. In my mind I pictured flames shooting out from all the windows. Where were the fire trucks? My teacher kept saying, "It's not real, it's just pretend, do not worry." The other children looked uncomfortable and confused by my reaction, but I was inconsolable. I could see the flames, why could nobody else? In the end, my mother had to come for me.

I remember it vividly. Growing up, I wondered why I reacted that way. Up until I was well into my twenties, I did not know how much I had blocked out about the plane crash. I never made the connection because I did not remember how much flying scared me. I did not know why we drove or took trains whenever it was possible. I never understood why we had to endure terminally long car rides every summer vacation. I had no idea that it was mostly because of me. And then, when I did start flying again at age twelve, oddly enough I really enjoyed it. I had so totally blocked the air crash that I barely thought about it, until I got older and it started to creep back into my consciousness. One night I was listening when my parents were telling some people about it. It was then I knew why I had been so terrified that day in Rangoon. I have always had a fear of fire. I used to tell people it was an irrational fear. But it was not—it is not.

If it happened today, I probably would have been sent to therapy. Somebody would have helped me process it. But in my family, we were always told to just get over it. To push through. To move on. There were things we just had to do, whatever it took. I guess blocking it all out was my way of being able to keep going.

In Rangoon we lived in a large one-story house on University Avenue with a big front yard, a horseshoe driveway, and a view of Inya Lake. We had a cook, a housekeeper, and my nanny, Mary, who had been with us in Pyinmana. When we first arrived, I asked my father who all those people were in our house. "They are here to help Virginia with the housework, cooking, cleaning, laundry, and babysitting." I said I thought it was pretty silly.

Some of our household help lived with their families in a building behind our house. It looked out over the road below. I had a few friends in our neighborhood, but I also spent time playing with the children in our compound. In April, a very hot time of year, the Burmese celebrate the New Year with the Water Festival, which symbolizes a cleansing for the New Year. We would get buckets of water and sneak out back and throw water on to unsuspecting passersby. It was great fun. The Burmese were used to this tradition and usually did not mind getting drenched. I remember once an exquisitely dressed woman passed below our house. We were thrilled because she was an excellent target for our water bucket. As we discharged our ammunition, she amazingly opened her umbrella just in time. What a disappointment! My mother, however, hated that festival and avoided going out whenever possible.

In January 1962, a good friend of my parents', U Kyao, the forestry officer who had been stationed in Pyinmana, was put in charge of a large forest operation and elephant camp in the Kachin State. He invited several of us to spend a few days with him at his camp on Lake Indawgyi, about 120 miles southwest of Myitkyina, near the Chinese border.

I must have been about ten years old when I wrote this essay:

ELEPHANT CAMP

I went to an elephant camp in Burma. In this camp there are about 90 work elephants kept in a teak forest. They make expensive furniture out of teak. They also make the frame of ships out of teak wood. The elephants are used to either push or pull heavy teak logs to the river where the logs then float down to the city Rangoon.

When I went to elephant camp the thing I most enjoyed was riding an elephant. You sit in a wooden box, and you sort of sway from side to side and you could get seasick if you rode for very long and were not used to it. Most of you must think that elephants don't have hair, but my mother soon found out that they do have hair because she slid down the back of the elephant instead of climbing down on this head and front knee as she should have, and the strong hairs stuck to her pants. These hairs are black, they are about four inches long and they are very strong.

We fed the elephants the fruit from the tamarind trees. Tamarind is an acidy brown fruit which the elephants like very much.

Each elephant has its own caretaker, and rider called an oozie in Burmese. This man feeds and takes good care of his elephant. He also carves out of wood a bell which the elephant always wears around his neck. Every night the elephant is set free to find food in the forest. In the morning when the oozie goes to find his elephant he knows which one is his by the sound of the bell his elephant is wearing.

We spent four days at this camp up near the China border and we learned much about elephants and teak wood.

According to my mother's letters we flew to Myitkyina with a stop in Mandalay. The roads in Burma were generally not good and there were still insurgents floating around, so flying was often the safest option.

To get to the forestry camp from Myitkyina, we drove over thirty-eight miles of the old Ledo Road, which was still a good road. The Ledo Road, also known as the Stilwell Road, was an overland connection between British India and China, built during World War II to enable the Western Allies to deliver supplies to China and aid the war effort against Japan.

At the camp, we stayed in a barrack-like building where we slept on cots under mosquito nets. I remember the building was far from the outhouse; at night we had to go with a flashlight down a rutted mud road—very scary for a five-year-old but a big adventure all the same.

During the day we rode for miles through deep jungle and watched elephants at work hauling timber to the river where it flowed downstream. A highlight of the trip was that one of the elephants had just given birth to twins, a very rare event; we spent hours watching them play.

My mother wrote in a letter to her mother:

> It poured rain the night before we left elephant camp, so our trip back was terrifying over the first 30 miles—muddy narrow, slippery, no-barrier mountain road. But we made it (4-wheel drive jeeps are truly wonderful!). Next day we drove to Bhamo through gorgeous scenery and had supper in a Chinese cafe in Bhamo (they brought us boiling water to dip our dishes and chopsticks in before using them) you would be horrified to eat in such a place, but the food was delicious and hot and we were starved.

That evening we boarded a riverboat to go down the Irrawaddy River to Mandalay. The boat had a small cabin area upstairs with berths, but the bottom was open air, with people packed on to it like sardines.

The boat stopped occasionally so people could get on and off, which gave us a chance to visit a village or buy something from peddlers. We quickly decided that exiting the vessel was not worth the trouble because we had to either wade off the boat or try our luck on the treacherous plank. There were six people in our group, and everybody dined with the British captain in his private dining room except me because I was too young to be allowed to sit with the adults, according to British custom. All I remember eating were vanilla wafers and Lipton's dried tomato soup. Yum.

THE EXIT

In March 1962, General Ne Win led a coup d'état and took over Burma. Within several months all foreigners were asked to leave. My mother wrote to her family:

> April 16, 1962, Rangoon
>
> This government has decided to not take any more help from Foundations—no reasons are given at all and the PM won't even see people concerned. So this means we will close out and be leaving sometime before October probably. Nothing settled about that because we haven't heard from NY (a bit of a shock to them, no doubt!). Anyhow, it doesn't affect us so much but we feel so badly about all the local people who are appreciating and recognizing the help. This is a top level decision only, we know, and no one seems to understand it. So far it is being kept very quiet, they say they want us to just fade away—finish existing projects and leave. At least, it is interesting to see what will happen. It has been a possibility of course since the coup, so we were not too surprised, but many others are and will be.
>
> Bill will have to wait till others (about 7 families) get gone. Where we'll go, we have no idea—that also will depend possibly on the NY office. The Asia Foundation,

> Fullbright program and much of the British Council program have also been curtailed.
>
> Love, Virginia

The July 7 Student Uprising was in reaction to the new military regime and the changes put in place on the Rangoon University campus. About 5,000 students protested over the course of two days. The military moved in to shut down the protest. At least one-hundred students were killed and most everybody else were arrested. The military blew up the Rangoon University student union the next day and closed the university.

> July 11, 1962
>
> Peninsula Hotel, Kowloon, Hong Kong
>
> We gratefully left Burma yesterday noon and arrived here about 4 hours later. Saying goodbye was sad in the case of many of our friends, but at the moment we are not too sorry to leave the country. You have probably read of the trouble at the University, and people just don't know what the outcome will be nor what may happen next. Many cried at our leaving—not so much a personal thing but so many are exiting now!
>
> Love, Virginia

Ne Win ruled for nearly twenty-six years and during that time, Burma went from being the breadbasket of Asia and a main exporter of rice to one of the most impoverished nations in the world. To this day, the Burmese people struggle for freedom and human rights.

My father was always curious about the Agricultural Institute he started in Burma and wanted to know if it survived given the difficult times Burma was experiencing. In 1971 he was able to get a visa and go for a visit. He arrived almost nineteen years to the day from his first arrival in Burma.

Not much had changed in Burma since he had left. The only difference he noted was that the train to Pyinmana ran on time and live chickens were no longer allowed in the compartments. The countryside and villages looked the same.

When the institute started, there were four Burmese professional staff members and my father. In 1971, the staff numbered twenty-four, and twenty of those were former students of his, most of whom had gone abroad after finishing at Pyinmana to obtain their degrees either in the Philippines or the United States. Over 800 students had graduated from the institute and the student body included a number of women.

As of 2004, the institute had evolved into a full four-year college of agriculture and had over 2,000 graduates. It is still going strong to this day.

RYE, NEW YORK 1962

After three days in Taipei, and a few days in Tokyo (where I got my beautiful Japanese doll that I loved for years afterward), the family flew to San Francisco and then drove to Los Angeles to see family and on to Shenandoah, Iowa, and Lodi, Wisconsin. My father went to New York City to discuss things with the Ford Foundation and found a house to rent in Rye, New York. Then everybody, including my grandparents, Fern and Harry, drove to New York and arranged for the furniture from storage in Ithaca to be shipped down. Fern and Harry helped move us in. Harry wanted to see the ocean and taste the water to see if it was really salty. We went to Jones Beach where he could walk out into the water and taste it. Yes, it was salty. Confirmed. He was happy.

We lived in Rye for almost a year, and I went to first grade within walking distance of our house. I had been in a small international school in Rangoon where everybody knew me and my family. In Rye I was to attend a large public school. My parents took me with them to meet the principal and I was introduced to my teacher before I started school. After I had gone for a few days, I refused to go back. I would not go. Nobody in my family could make me.

My mother called the principal to tell him I refused to go to school. His response was, "You have to send her to school, it's the law!" My mother tried to explain to him that they wanted me to go but I refused. Eventually they got the reason out of me. Even though I had met the principal before, he had not greeted me when he passed me in the hallway. Plus, when I went to my classroom, my teacher did not know my name. It was not acceptable to me. My brother was unsympathetic. He told me to get over myself.

My mother managed to get another meeting with the principal and took me in to see him. He apologized to me for not speaking to me in the hallway and my teacher took me aside and explained that she had a lot of students, and it took time to learn everybody's name. She did not forget my name after that.

In the summer of 1963, my father was offered a job in Mexico City, also working for the Ford Foundation. Since we had been in the States for less than a year, he was given the option to go to Mexico or stay in New York.

My father remembers: "We discussed as a family whether Tim, Tom and Kathy wanted to change schools and move again, especially since Tim had only one year more in high school. They all said, 'Let's go to Mexico.' By this time, Tim had applied to college under the early decision program (where a well-qualified applicant can gain early acceptance). I started taking Spanish lessons. The New York newspapers all stopped circulation due to a strike, so I started using the one-hour commute to and from work to study Spanish."

There would be no airplanes involved—we took the train.

PART TWO

MEXICO CITY 1963

I turned seven in the summer of 1963. After visiting relatives in the Midwest, we boarded the train in Kansas City bound for Mexico. My main travel concern was for my pet turtle, Tootsie. I put Tootsie in a peanut butter jar and poked holes in the top. It was summer, and as we reached the border at Laredo, Texas, it must have been at least 100 degrees. The air conditioning went out…well, not so much went out as turned off. Or maybe we changed to a train without it. It happened just as we crossed over the border into Mexico and it was sweltering. Desert heat. Dry, hot, no air, and the sun beating down. We opened the windows but there was no breeze.

We sat sweating on the train for a while and eventually everybody had to get off for the customs inspection. Tootsie was in my mother's carry-on bag, which was now on top of a table in the middle of the cavernous customs house. The uniformed official walked up and down and around this table eyeing the luggage. He briefly looked as if he was going to inspect the carry-on bag. We all held our breath. Lucky for me, in the end I managed to successfully smuggle a live turtle across the border undetected by customs. When we reached Mexico City, I spent the entire day looking over my shoulder expecting to be nabbed for my illegal import. They never caught up with me and Tootsie lived a full turtle life (or at least another year or two).

When we first arrived, we lived in a temporary house in outer suburbia. It was a gated neighborhood called El Pedregal, meaning "rocky garden." The area was one big lava field with black chunks of lava everywhere. We had to climb up the stairs over them to get into the house. The houses did not have yards, just lava with trees and some flowers. It was far enough out of town that you could see the snow-capped volcanoes on a very clear day—though those were rare in Mexico City. It sits in a valley surrounded by mountains, so all the smog just hangs in the basin and chokes everybody. At an elevation of 7,600 feet the air is thin. All of this took some getting used to.

Not too long after we arrived, my father was off on a business trip and my mother and I were alone in the house with the maids, who spoke no English. Suddenly, they became very upset and came to my mother's room to tell her something. We did not speak Spanish yet and could not understand what they were saying. They kept saying "Kennedy! Kennedy!" and then pretended to shoot a gun. We gathered that the president had been shot but we could not determine if he was dead or not. Later in the day, another expat wife was kind enough to phone my mother and fill her in that our president, John F. Kennedy, was dead. It was a Friday. Monday was a day of mourning. Schools and businesses were closed. JFK was very popular in Mexico.

My mother wrote to her parents:

November 25, 1963

Today is quite a day of mourning here, too. The children's schools were closed, many businesses closed, and four or more memorial services held—a Catholic one in the big Cathedral of Guadalupe (where Kennedys had visited), a Greek Orthodox one, a protestant one in Episcopal church and a Jewish one in the synagogue—at least. We have been informed, though not always as quickly as we would like! Agustina told me of it first in Spanish, but we can't get an American radio station till dark and we can't understand the radio in Spanish enough to know what's going on (our shortwave radio is in storage here in the city, of course!). A friend did call to tell us the barest details. Then yesterday Agustina again told us about Oswald's being shot, but our radio batteries (all three transistors) had run down, so we had to wait for today's paper to get the details of that. It's all quite awful, but history in the making, and somehow I think Johnson will be a good president. We all went to church yesterday even though I have had a terrible cold. This morning, I got Tom and Kath up and breakfasted when we found their school was closed. So we all went to the supermarket, then I had my hair done and now Tom is trying to write a speech to give in Spanish for tomorrow and Tim and Kathy are "helping" him!

Love, Virginia

In this new city I had the choice of going to the American school, which was very large and, well, American, and Greengates, the British school, which was much smaller. One of my brothers and I chose the British school, while my eldest brother went to the American school.

The British school was in two big houses with connected lots in a residential area. There were several outbuildings scattered around a central assembly area. Every morning, we would line up by class and listen to whatever announcements were relevant and then we were dismissed by class to our classrooms. The teachers all came to us. Every Wednesday afternoon we had sports. We would get onto buses and travel to the YMCA or some other club to go swimming or play soccer or do track and field. Everybody wore a uniform of grey pants or skirt, white shirt, green blazer, and green tie. I liked never having to think about what to wear. The headmaster, Mr. Coehlo, was a very strict Britisher. I do not know why he was in Mexico or much else about him, but he ran a tight ship. There were three main forms of punishment: a wrap (or several) on the knuckles with a ruler, the writing of lines, and suspension/expulsion. Some teachers would get very creative and compose whole paragraphs for line writing. Then we would have to copy it twenty, thirty, or fifty times. Or more. It was more time-consuming than anything else.

Unfortunately, because I was behind in certain areas since I was coming from a different system, they put me in the first grade again. It was my third time in first grade, or Form I, as the British called it. Before we were asked to leave Burma, I had just started first grade there. In New York, I went to public school and completed first grade. Now I was there again, feeling awful. I was trying to maneuver a new country, a new language, new people, a new school and now I had to play catch-up. I studied, studied, worried, and studied some more; then halfway through the year they put me in second grade. They just pulled me out of class one day and said, "We are moving you to Form II." The Form I students were in school only until noon and then caught the bus home. From then on, I stayed until 2 PM. When they pulled me out of class, I about had a panic attack because I was sure I would miss my bus.

I was so obsessed with doing well, I ended second grade at the top of my class and even received an award. I did not want to be the dumb kid and not fit in. I was top of my class until the fourth grade and for a year, I woke up every morning with a stomachache. My mother took me to all kinds of doctors, but nobody knew why I had a stomachache. Finally, they realized it was nerves and said I had the beginning of an ulcer and that I should learn to relax. I was nine years old.

Even though I was diagnosed with nerves, I really did like Greengates. That same year, Prince Philip came to visit our school and spoke to us at assembly. A friend and I went to watch him play polo and afterward, we went up to him, shook his hand and introduced ourselves. He was charming and friendly. We were very excited, giggly seven-year-olds, curtseying as best we could in our jeans.

The students came from twenty-seven different countries. We usually travelled in packs and spoke a mixture of Spanish and English. Many kids spoke a third language at home. When we talked to each other we would use the words that first popped into our head or that were the most appropriate for their meaning, it did not matter what language it was. However, if we spoke anything but English at school, we would get into trouble.

One day during the first year at my new school, I arrived in the morning and walked through the gates into the foyer. Everybody was buzzing and there were whispers all around. The young ones were especially giggly and excited. I wondered what was going on.

Although the name of the school was Greengates, the gates were black. My mother always joked that somebody should paint them green. And in fact, that morning, somebody had painted them green. My brother and his friends were called into the headmaster's office and expelled for a week because they were the guilty ones. I did not know whether to be ashamed or proud. He is still a legend there. Of course, part of their punishment was to paint the gates black.

I met Lisa in the third grade and she was my best friend until she moved away in the sixth grade. She spent a lot of time at my house because she always wanted to get away from her annoying sisters and overbearing father. Her parents were Polish immigrants to the US, but she had been born in Connecticut. She was more American than the Americans. She had every board game and the very latest Barbie dolls with all the accessories. She had an Easy-Bake Oven that we could make real cakes in, a Creepy Crawlers kit that had molds for making plastic creatures, every Beatles album, and every other latest gadget. Whenever her father went to the US, he brought home the latest consumer items. The things they had crammed into their closets always fascinated me.

Years later, I ran into Lisa when her parents had just been posted to Paris. I was in boarding school in Switzerland at the time and in love with Europe. She hated living in Paris and wanted to be back in New York. She ended up back in the States, finishing high school there while living with a friend's family. I never understood how she could give up Paris for some suburban US high school. Maybe it was just too hard for her to say goodbye to friends and start over.

When I was in the fourth grade I sat next to Robbie Dean. He was a ladies' man at nine years old and gave me a "ruby" ring one day on the bus (I still have it). We bickered all the time, but people thought we were in love and one day the whole class started singing "Robbie and Kathy, sitting in a tree, k-i-s-s-i-n-g…." The teacher had been out of the room and came back furious because of all the noise. We were all made to write lines. I protested because it was so unfair to be completely humiliated and then be punished. Life can be a real bitch.

LAS LOMAS

After spending six months in outer suburbia, we moved closer to town in the neighborhood known as Las Lomas. *Lomas* translates as "hills." Across the street from us was a barranca which was like a huge ditch or ravine. We lived in a fairly modern, two-story house with four bedrooms. We did not completely get away from the lava, though. The wall that surrounded our house was made of lava rock. Across the street was an estate where the owner of a big Mexican brewery lived, and we could see swans swimming in his little lake. The famous comedian Cantinflas lived up the street from us and I even saw him a couple of times, whizzing by in his swanky car.

We shared a walled-in compound with our landlady who lived in an identical house. Doña Isabel, the landlady, always kept dogs, mainly for security reasons and because she had a weakness for collies. Because the only thing separating us was a hedge, the dogs spent most of their time at our house. We gave them lots of attention while she basically ignored them. The dogs, Scout and Mitzi, always barked their heads off if anybody approached the gates, so she did not mind if we enjoyed them as pets. My father never allowed us to have actual pets when we lived in the city. He had grown up on a farm and was adamant that animals belonged outside. Except for my turtle, of course.

Our next-door neighbors on the other side, were a Mexican family with eight children. We had a chain-link fence between us covered with ivy growing on it but there was one section we could see through, and we would hang out and talk through the fence. They invited me on family outings with them. The whole family were nuts for playing dominoes so I would go over to their house and play dominoes for hours. The mother had lived in Texas and spoke perfect English and most of the kids spoke English as well. There was one boy my age and one a bit older. When I was about thirteen, I had my first real crush on the older one. I went all tingly whenever we held hands. When I moved away, we wrote to each other for a while, and he taped my letters to his bedroom wall. His sisters laughed and laughed when they saw that and teased him endlessly. Poor guy. I think that was what put an end to our 'relationship.' I caught up with him about fifty years later and we had a nice chat. Unfortunately, he died of cancer soon after that. I am still in touch with one of his sisters.

We had lots of visitors when we lived in Mexico. The proximity to the US made it easy for friends and family to come, plus there were always my father's work-related visitors popping in and out. July was the dry season, and we would usually go for a week or two where nothing came out of the tap. We had a big water tank under our stairway outside that would run dry. This often happened when we had people visiting. My mother loved it because it showed them that our life was not as glamorous as everyone assumed.

My parents entertained a lot. Whenever we had parties, it meant I could stay up late. I always "mingled" and helped serve hors d'oeuvres. All kinds of people came through our house. I remember one man who had the funniest name. I could not understand why he had a "Mc" in front of his first name and for a long time I called McGeorge Bundy, McGeorge McBundy because I thought it sounded better that way. Bundy was president of the Ford Foundation at the time.

Most of the time we lived in Las Lomas we had a cook and a maid and a gardener. Josefina, our cook, stayed with us the entire time we lived in Mexico. We had several different maids and by the time we left we only had a temporary maid who would come in two or three times a week. Josefina taught me how to cook quesadillas and *cajeta* (also known as dulce de leche) and she always had a fresh stack of tortillas in the refrigerator that she would heat over a gas burner and smear with butter for a snack. She doubled as a babysitter, and we would watch TV together at night when my parents were out. After she had been with us for a few years, she told my mother she had a son who was living in her village and wanted to know if he could come and visit her. My mother was taken aback. In Asia (and in Africa too) the children of the household help often lived with them in the compound. Josefina's son Jaime came to live with us when he was about seven.

Mexico was really the country of my youth. The first chunk of my third culture was formed there. I absorbed the language. The bright colors of the gardens and the flowers and the art and the markets and the clothing all became a part of me. To this day color makes me happy. The smell of warm tortillas and corn and mole and different chilis all take me right back to Mexico. The street vendors selling fresh warm chicharron with lime and chili. The man with the ice cream freezer on wheels selling popsicles: lime, mango, coconut, pineapple, strawberry. Beef grilling in the open air. Orange Fanta. Mariachi bands playing at Christmas parties. Bullfights. Bargaining at the open market. Perusing the Bazar Sabado (the Art Bazaar). Paddle boats in Chapultepec Park. Riding bikes in the park. *Pesero* taxis. All these things are still part of me.

SNAPSHOTS FROM MEXICO

ACAPULCO

It's about an eight-hour drive to Acapulco from Mexico City. We did it every year on the day after Christmas. I remember the hot sand and the ocean breeze. Body surfing and being churned up and spit out onto a rough beach—I still have scars. Getting sunburned from living in my bathing suit. Hanging by the pool and ordering tacos. Drinking cokes. Playing Mini Golf. Walking on the beach at night. It was heaven.

When my oldest brother graduated college, he got drafted because of the Vietnam War and was able to come home for Christmas before they sent him overseas. At that point, he did not know where they were going to send him, but he had to fly out of the airport in Acapulco to get back to base on time. I thought he was very brave to do that. None of the rest of us had ever flown out of there—we always drove to Acapulco.

TEOTIHUACÁN (TEH-OH-TEE-WAH-KAHN)

First the Sun Pyramid was excavated, now known to be the third largest pyramid in the world. This is where they sacrificed virgins, cut their hearts out, and offered them to the gods. It made me nervous being up there—I was a virgin. Then the Moon Pyramid was excavated. Then there were more excavations: a butterfly gallery, the Temple of Quetzalcóatl. Snake heads poked out of the rubble. Slowly a city emerged, hot, dusty, and vast.

POPOCATÉPETL AND IXTACCIHUATL

To the south are two snowcapped volcanoes. Popo still erupts from time to time. One of the Aztec legends is that Popo and Ixta fell in love, but she was a princess, and he was a common soldier. Her father said the only way they could get married was if he went to war and came back victorious. Off he went. One of his enemies reported back to Ixta that Popo had died in battle, and she soon died of sorrow. When Popo returned victorious to find her dead, he carried her into the mountains and laid her to rest where he could watch over her for eternity. They are beautiful mountains, but they always made me sad because of the story.

CUERNAVACA

Then there were the Sunday drives down the mountain to Cuernavaca. Being young, I only have flashes of memory of this time. Warm sunshine. Lower altitude. Begonia. Marigold. Hibiscus. Bougainvillea. Colors everywhere. Fragrant. Sitting in the garden at Las Mañanitas hotel and restaurant. Watching the peacocks and parrots wandering around. Fish swimming in the fountain. One time I watched a man eat baby eels. He ate the eels with their little eyes staring out at me. I was transfixed. *Yuck!*.

SWIMMING

Then there was Veracruz. Too hot for words. Cooling off in the ocean. Loving the waves. A man off in the distance yelling, "*Tiburón! Tiburón!*" Desperately paddling for shore. Sharks? No, thank you!

Then the Fortín de las Flores. A pool full of gardenias. Overwhelming fragrance of gardenias. They got in the way of swimming. Why would they mess with my day that way?

And the Hacienda Vista Hermosa. Pool after pool connected under archways and waterfalls spilling around. Shallow pools full of people. Floating on a hot day.

GOATS

We visited a hacienda in the Mexican countryside. We had a tour of the farm and afterwards we were invited to have lunch with the family (the midday meal is always the largest in Mexico). My father was the guest of honor, so he sat to the right of the head of the household, don Alvaro.

The main thing I remember eating that day was cabrito for the first time. Cabrito is baby goat meat and it is delicious. We had soup first and then they brought out the main course. A woman came out and placed a plate in front of my father. Because he was the guest of honor, he received the goat's head—the skull with eyes and brains in it. I just sat there and watched, wondering what he would do.

He sat in silence for a few minutes looking at the thing and then he turned to don Alvaro and said, "I thank you very much for this honor, but I am sure that you would appreciate this delicacy more than I," and handed over the plate. Of course, don Alvaro was thrilled and devoured the whole thing with gusto. I was amazed, but that's the kind of guy my dad was. Always able to cope with any situation with grace and style.

EARTHQUAKES

Sometimes I would wake up in the middle of the night and sit up in bed, unsure what was happening. I could see the hanging light in my room swaying. It was an earthquake! Eventually, since it happened often, I learned to go back to sleep. They usually happened at night or in the morning. One morning there was a pretty big one—7.3 on the Richter scale. I was sitting at the breakfast table and the room started to shake. My father immediately got up and ran out into the yard. My mother was climbing the stairs and did not feel a thing. I sat mesmerized by the water in my glass swaying back and forth. I think people were able to trick themselves because living in a place where earthquakes happen so often they felt normal, not unusual. You just could not worry about it.

PALACIO DE BELLAS ARTES

Mexico City was built on top of a lake so many of the older buildings were sinking. The Palacio de Bellas Artes was a fabulous art deco building that had sunk about thirteen feet. You would go down to get into it instead of up. It was the home of the Mexican Ballet Folklorico, which celebrated the diversity of regional Mexican cultures through dance. If we got there early, we could see the Tiffany glass curtain that portrayed the two volcanoes Popo and Ixta. The whole time I lived in Mexico I took ballet lessons and every year the Russian Bolshoi Ballet would come to town and perform at the Bellas Artes Theater. I was lucky enough to go more than once. And when I lived in Moscow many years later, it was a very special experience to go to the actual Bolshoi Theatre.

BULLFIGHTS

One thing my family enjoyed, which is now kind of controversial, was bullfights. My mother remembers her first bullfight:

> February 1965
>
> We had good seats on the sunny side quite near the ring and the sun felt good. It was, as always, a colorful pageant with the matadors, banderilleros, and picadors all wearing such fancy beautiful suits, just like the pictures we have seen. A brass band played in interludes and at the time two very regal sounding trumpets announced the actual fights. Twice the matadors did such a good job they paraded around the ring and people threw down flowers, hats, and flasks from which the matadors drank, and scarves that they put on and then threw back. The bulls were not very ferocious that day, so the crowd was quite disgruntled. A horse was gored

quite badly. Surprisingly though, I did not mind the bulls getting slain—as Kathy said, it was so ugly and bad that she enjoyed the killing of it the most. The best part of it, for me, was when the three brightly decorated mules with snappy little men in blue uniforms and a wheelbarrow, shovels and brooms, come out in a great flourish and dragged the dead bull out of the ring and cleaned up any blood. It was an absolute riot to see them. The mules were balky, and the crowd would alternately boo and clap, enjoying it as much as the fight, I do believe.

Also, as is always true in crowds, the audience was most interesting, and as the beer flowed freely so the audience relaxed and enjoyed themselves and you should hear Kathy yell, 'Olé!' We all enjoyed it.

I was in love with El Cordobés, one of the greatest bullfighters of all time. I had a poster of him on my bedroom wall. He was from Cordoba, Spain. We often went to the arena to watch the bullfights, but we also gathered around the television to watch them on Sunday afternoons. My brother Tim's eighteenth birthday present was tickets to the bullfight to see El Cordobés. That day the matador was rewarded with two ears, a tail, and a hoof for his performance. This was an accomplishment that was unheard of. He also was paraded down Reforma, the city's main street. I was so jealous that my brother got to see it!

GUATEMALA AND EL SALVADOR 1968

My first plane trip in many years was in the first-class section on a Pan American Airways flight from Mexico to Guatemala when I was twelve. We were the only ones in first class so I got to be kind of chummy with the flight attendant. Toward the end of the flight, he asked me how I liked the flight and how I felt about it. I thought that was kind of an odd question and did not know what he was talking about. Apparently, my parents had briefed him on me and my troubles with flying, and so he made a special effort to distract me. It had been six years since I was on a plane and seven years since the crash. By this time I was aware I had been in a plane crash, but I had no memory of habitually getting physically ill or screaming before getting on an airplane. I had actually enjoyed this flight but since he brought it to my attention, I did start to wonder why it was a big deal. It made me start to ask some questions, but my parents never wanted to talk about it and would brush my questions aside.

In Guatemala, we rented a car and drove up the mountain to Lake Atitlán. It was large at over fifty square miles, and one of the most beautiful lakes in the world. Surrounded by volcanoes, the lake itself is a collapsed volcanic caldera formed over 80,000 years ago. The combination of mountains and water are always thrilling to me. Lake Atitlán has been compared to Lake Como in Italy, another beautiful place with surrounding mountains. The people who lived in the area were of

Mayan origin. On our way up the mountain, we saw people lying by the side of the road. We did not know if they were dead, passed out, or taking a nap. It was very odd. We later found out that the previous day was payday, and they had done their celebrating and not quite made it home. Apparently, it was a familiar sight in the countryside. We stopped in Chichicastenango to see the large popular market and the Catholic church built on a Mayan temple before arriving in Antigua.

This was major earthquake country. Antigua was the original capital of Guatemala built in the 1500's. In the mid 1700's the Santa Marta earthquakes were the final straw. After years and years of major earthquakes, the capital was finally moved to where it is today—Guatemala City. There was a new part of Antigua and an old part. The old part was nestled under three volcanoes. The Volcán de Agua was inactive (12,336 ft.), the Volcán de Fuego was quite active (12,362 ft.), and the Volcán de Acatenango was active from time to time (13,045 ft.). The old part of the city was all ruins. It was an eerie place, empty and abandoned. The fallen buildings looked like skeletons, and it felt like the place was full of ghosts. It was once a major city that tumbled down and was left there like a memorial. We stopped at a small restaurant in the new part of town and ate our meal outside in the yard. There was a group of musicians that wandered from table to table. We could see laundry hanging on a line at the end of the lawn.

From there, we continued to El Salvador. One night in San Salvador we were staying in a high-rise hotel and I was sleeping on a cot. The building started to sway, and my cot started moving across the room—it was an earthquake. I probably should have taken it more seriously, but after all the earthquakes I had lived through, all I could do was laugh.

AUSTIN 1969

When I finished the seventh grade, my parents felt it was time for me to go into the American system. Most of my good friends were going off to boarding school in England or other places or transferring to the American School. The American School in Mexico City had been my rival school up until then and I really had no desire to go there. My brothers had gone away to boarding school when they were nine and eleven and I always tried to keep up with them as much as I could, so I chose boarding school.

Growing up in Mexico, we would usually spend summer vacations with relatives in the Midwest. My mother's family lived in Wisconsin, and we would shuffle back and forth between my grandmother's apartment and my aunt's house. I was always camped out on somebody's couch. I had cousins to play with and American TV to watch. We went swimming and played softball and went shopping. My siblings and I also had to go for our annual medical checkups, which I dreaded every year.

When I was nine, I went off to camp for four weeks in northern Minnesota. Most people went for two weeks. I was the only one who stayed for four—besides the counselors. Camp was everything I loved: swimming in the lake, being in the woods, playing tennis, riding horses, canoeing, and sailing. I was there to have fun and learn new things. I was excited to go. I had some adjustment problems, but the counselors were nice, and we were kept so busy, people did not have a lot of time to harass each other. I remember kids would ask me where I was from and I would say, "I live in Mexico." They would respond, "Oh, really? Where in New Mexico do you live?" Then I would have to explain to them that Mexico is a country. It annoyed me to have to even discuss it. Who cared where I was from? I did not care where they were from. Weren't we all Americans? I did not make a lot of friends mostly because I was "different." After the third year it was not fun anymore. As we got into our teens, the girls got mean and cliquey. It was not about having fun in the woods, but became more about who you were and where you came from. Many of them came from wealthy families in Iowa. I just could not relate.

My mother tried to instill one value in me about America that has always stuck with me and made me glad I had an American passport. She explained what made America great and different from most countries was that everybody had the right to voice their opinion and fight for their ideas, hopes, and dreams. She thought this caused continual change and change was good because it kept things fresh and young and in turn encouraged new ideas. Although sometimes, the changes were not all that great.

One thing I understood at a young age in Mexico was *la mordida*, which literally means "the bite." It was never called a bribe, just a little gift for services. Whenever I would witness a *mordida* to a policeman or a customs official, my mother would tell me that in the US such things never happened and if anybody were to try that, they would be arrested on the spot. I grew up with a horrible fear of American police. I was scared I would do something that seemed perfectly normal to me, like offer them money or even jaywalk and they would throw me in jail.

Since I had chosen boarding school, when I was thirteen I started at St. Stephen's Episcopal School in Austin, Texas. This would be my fifth school. Luckily, there were quite a few people like me whose parents lived overseas. The school was on 370 acres overlooking Lake Austin. We had to drive about five miles on a winding one-lane back road to get there from the main highway out of Austin. It felt remote with a pretty, natural setting, but they had most everything a high school needed: playing fields, a swimming pool, tennis courts, a big gym, a library, a cafeteria, dorms, classrooms, and other recreational areas. And of course there was also a big church. Church was mandatory twice a week. There were lots of rules. A big bell woke us up in the morning. Everybody had a job. Since I was in the youngest class, I was always given the worst jobs, like sweeping, emptying trash, and waiting on tables. Meals were mandatory. I had to go to study hall in the evenings. At night I had to be inside the dorm at a certain time and then it was lights out. I was forever signing "in" or "out," since they kept track of your every minute.

Most of the kids were very tuned in to the times and I realized how out of touch I had been living overseas. I knew nothing about the '60s revolution or about any of the current American music or culture. All I had heard were the Beatles, the Rolling Stones, and the Monkees. So when I was asked if I wanted to go to a Janis Joplin concert, I said, "Who's she?"

In October 1969, I went to see Janis Joplin in concert. She wore a black see-through outfit and she had a bottle of Jack Daniels sitting on the piano. She drank most of it over the course of the evening. She was hot. She belted out her songs and enjoyed every minute of her time on the stage. She flirted with all the guys in the front row. The drunker she got, the more she flirted—but the singing did not suffer. I thought she was amazing. I had never seen anything like it. We had seats in the rafters and that night was the first time I was kissed by a boy, on the lips. It was quite a night to remember.

My freshman year, I made the tennis team. The star of the team was a girl whose father was a well-known high official in the Johnson administration. She and I used to take off into the bushes after practice to have a cigarette. The only thing was, she never got caught. I got caught one day and ended up getting kicked off the tennis team, which of course freed up my time to go into the bushes and smoke more cigarettes.

Adolescence is always a growing process and can be filled with insecurity and despair. I went through a very negative phase in Texas. I hated the authority that was always breathing down my neck. I felt that I was being suppressed and unable to express myself. The teachers were not friendly people who you could talk to and discuss your classes with or your problems. They became the enemy, people to be avoided at all costs. At first, I would not cooperate in class. I would not do their every command; I was going to be my own person. But after a while, I realized the only way I would survive was to give them what they wanted. I found that if I played their game, they would leave me alone. They no longer badgered me with questions or called me into offices for lectures. They acted like they had accomplished a great thing. I had progressed. I did have one teacher who was decent. I loved to write poetry. It was my therapy, my outlet. My history teacher realized this and appreciated it. He let me write my poetry instead of tedious papers that spit back what he had said. Poetry was my salvation there. I would write down my innermost feelings and then I would feel a little better:

Why?

Why is it like this?

Why can it not change?

I guess there is a reason somewhere

But I can't find it.

If it must be this way I

Would like to crawl into a hole

And stay until it all passes by

How?

On beautiful days

Such ugly happiness

All of it is true

And from here I see no end

Always hoping for the best
And you end up
Starting another day
Of the same thing
Why?

Life bothered me, too. I felt very insignificant in a world that did not make much sense. I wondered about human nature. How do people get to be the way they are? Why can't the world live in peace? Why can't we accept each other as we are? Why must there be so much conformity, so much hatred, so much thirst for power, so much dominance?

My second year in Texas, I had been back for two weeks when I found myself standing in a boy's room with about five boys. This was definitely not allowed. No way could a girl be in a boy's dorm. I had my back to the door, and I was showing them a card trick. I heard a voice behind me say, "What are you doing in here?" I did not move. I looked up at one of the boy who was facing the door and he had a look of horror on this face. Again the voice said, "What are you doing in here?" I turned around very slowly and found myself face-to-face with the teacher in charge of the boys dorms. I told him I was showing these guys a card trick. The response was, "Get out of here!" I walked back to my dorm and was telling a friend about my experience when the woman in charge of my dorm, Mrs. Wolf, came storming in with a shocked look on her face and blurted out "Whatever possessed you to do such a thing?" Well, I did not see what I had done as such a criminal act. It was not like we were having a wild orgy or anything, but I decided to keep my mouth shut. My punishment was that I could not leave campus for two weeks. More confinement.

Days go by
The same things happen
The weather gets worse
The weather gets better

Days go by
You do wrong things
To liven it up
And get in trouble
If you didn't do wrong things
You would go insane
For the boredom invades you
And you get in trouble
And
Days go by
The same things happen

While in Texas I started taking art lessons in the evenings in order to get out of study hall. I had no idea I would love it so much. I started to paint, with acrylics, bright colors on large canvases. We learned how to build and stretch our own canvas. We learned how to prime the canvas. I painted landscapes and color combinations. My teacher thought I was influenced by all my years of living in Mexico and all the bright colors that are ever-present in that country. Color was my trademark. I continue to paint and draw to this day.

One thing that was very much a part of that time was drugs. It was a time of rebellion and experimentation. We wanted to be a part of it. We did not want to be just another body taking up space. We were looking for some sort of meaning for our existence. I was trying to deal with my inner self and cope with my depression. Nature always had a great influence on me: the weather, trees, flowers. I was relating to nature and to art instead. Although I did not get into drugs, I was still affected by it all. My roommate turned to drugs. She tried everything and one night she took LSD and a teacher found her wandering around campus.

I finished out that year without my roommate and my good friend, but I managed to survive. By that time, my parents had moved to Bogotá, Colombia and decided it would be good for me to live at home for a while. It was hard for me to leave my friends behind, but I had no regrets about leaving boarding school in Texas. I think the adjustment problems I had in Texas had less to do with my TCK background than with my age. For the most part, I could relate to my peers since many of them came from similar backgrounds.

Colombia meant yet another new school and new environment. I did not really look forward to having to make new friends, but it turned out to be easier than I thought.

THE BEACH 1971

My parents relocated to Bogotá, Colombia because my father had become the Ford Foundation Representative for Colombia and Venezuela. My parents had downsized from a two-story large four-bedroom house to a small one-story four-bedroom house. Most of our things were gone. My mother got rid of almost all the books, all my stuffed animals, my Barbie dolls, and I do not know what else. I could not blame her since she had to send everything air freight and could only send a limited amount. Looking back, it would have been nice if she had asked me but that never happened. But in truth they were not things I was particularly attached to at the time and I took it in stride. I just did not have the luxury of keeping things. I had to let go. There were a few things that ended up in a trunk and were my treasures that followed me around the world for a while, including my Japanese doll. Other than that, I did not have much.

At fifteen, I had just finished my freshman year in Texas. I would be going to the international school in Bogotá. It was good to be back in Latin America, with "my people"— expats, TCKs, people from all over; this was a culture I felt comfortable with.

At the time my parents were moving to Colombia there were major student riots at universities around the country. There were strong anti-American sentiments and students would pull people who had "official" or "foreigner" license plates out of their cars and then set the car on fire. My father said he would not move unless they provided him with a car with local plates that would not stand out. There were curfews in place for a while. Things had settled down by the time I arrived in summer of 1971. This was before the time of the big cartels and all the drug violence in Colombia.

The summer I arrived, my parents and I took a trip to the coast by car. My father was a beach fanatic and somebody in his office told him he would find the most beautiful pristine beaches imaginable at the coastal village of Tolú. Since he had to go to Cartagena on business anyway, he decided to make a trip of it and stop in Tolú and the resort town of Santa Marta as well. The trip was almost entirely through the Andes Mountains. These mountains hug the west coast of South America from Venezuela to the south of Chile over 5,500 miles. In Bogotá we lived in the mountains at 8,600 feet. It was an exciting trip with switchback turns, and sheer drop-offs with no guardrails. The mountains were impressive and the countryside lush and green. The drivers, however, were insane. They drove overloaded buses, passing trucks on curves at breakneck speed and pumping out exhaust fumes in the thin high-altitude air. It was all an adrenaline rush.

We stopped for a couple of days in Medellín, a city that was later known for its drug cartel. It was a small city built on the side of the mountains with a lot of old churches. My mother had a thing about Catholic churches. If there was a church anywhere nearby, we had to go see it. It was not a religious thing; it was a tourist thing. She wanted to see the architecture, the windows, and the statues. It used to really embarrass me to have to go into all these churches where people were praying just so we could snoop around.

The morning we left Medellín, we stopped at a small corner restaurant for breakfast. All we wanted was some orange juice, coffee, and rolls. I spoke Spanish fluently with no accent. My father spoke Spanish fluently but with an accent. We went up to the counter and I asked for three orange juices, *jugo de naranja*. Blank stares answered my simple request. I could not make them understand what I was saying. I had to resort to pointing and acting in order to get three orange juices. We decided that they saw so few foreigners they just assumed we did not speak Spanish and could not process the fact that we did. It was a strangely odd feeling to not be able to communicate. I was not used to it.

On the way down from the mountains, we had to follow a riverbed where much of the road had been washed away by flooding. The riverbed had cliffs going up on either side, with the river rushing quickly down the middle, and the road was off to one side. Where the road was washed out, there was no place else to go but *in* the river or hug the cliff. Fortunately, there was almost no traffic, and we were able to manage it, although we all had white knuckles as we passed through the mountains.

As we got to the coastal flatlands we started looking out for the road to Tolú. We were all very excited. The road turned out to be a narrow-rutted lane with overgrown plants and palm trees on either side. We said to ourselves, no problem, that this was good—it meant the town was unspoiled by the overuse of tourists. The village of Tolú was small. There was a square in the middle of town, but the main road was just past the center and ran along the ocean on the beach. Yes, the beach had become a road with buses barreling down it at high speeds. There were no swimmers or sunbathers—they would have died from the exhaust fumes first and a car accident second.

Since it was late in the day, we realized we had to stay the night, so we found a small hotel on the beach that looked passable. We were shown to a "suite" that had two rooms and five beds and a huge bathroom that only had cold water—and a million cockroaches. My father got up several times during the night to spray his mattress for bugs. We left early the next morning. When we got back to Bogotá my father told the person who had recommended Tolú all about our experience. Of course, the person had never actually been there. So much for pristine beaches. (I looked up Tolú recently and a tourist website says, "Tolú offers ecotourism ideal for diving and rain forest treks. The fishing town has now become a popular weekend and holiday destination for Colombian tourists, particularly those from Medellín." I guess things have changed. The photos look amazing.)

From Tolú we drove to Cartagena, the old Spanish outpost. There was a fort on the hill that had tunnels going down to the water. Niches were cut into the tunnel for soldiers to stand with their rifles and shoot people as they ran down the dark and claustrophobic tunnels. It all made me very uncomfortable. Cartagena had often been visited by pirates as well as by Spanish ships. They had set up a chain under the bay on one side to destroy any boats that were trying to sneak into the harbor. Those who did not know about the chain sank. Cartagena itself was a colorful touristy colonial town that felt very coastal and laid back. I liked it a lot.

Our next stop was Barranquilla, another big port and more of a bustling city. It was more of an industrial business center. Not really my favorite. Our final stop was Santa Marta, a small resort town near the Venezuelan border. Luckily, we flew home from Santa Marta, so we did not have to repeat the exciting mountain drive.

COLEGIO NUEVA GRANADA

My father travelled a lot while I grew up and even when at home he usually worked late at the office or went off to a social function. I saw very little of him. My mother often had headaches and always took a nap in the afternoon. Maybe it was the altitude or just her age. Bogotá was at 8,600 feet in the Andes Mountains. Lush and cool, it rained almost every day. The rain bothered my mother. She thought it was depressing, but I barely noticed it. Mostly left to my own devices, I was out and about, rain or shine.

Moving around so much meant constantly adapting and adjusting to new places and new people. After a while I became a chameleon, able to blend into any background. The last thing I ever wanted to do when moving to a new place was to stand out. I wanted it to look like I belonged where I was and that I knew what I was doing. I learned to hone my powers of observation, and I would spend the first few weeks in a new environment being reserved and quiet, watching everybody else. Then once I built up my confidence, I would break out like a phoenix, and my new persona would emerge, reinvented for my current surroundings. Constantly having to leave friends behind or see them leave me did take a toll and as I grew older, I became more discriminating about who I opened up to and became close to. In spite of that, I always looked forward to new places. It was an adventure, a challenge.

My uniform that year was a ruana (a wool cape) and a stiff felt men's hat that was very common among the native people who lived in the mountains. I also had a swell pair of suede lace-up boots and I wore rings on every finger. I also had long hair and long sharp nails; when I first arrived at school people thought I was some kind of witch. I loved it there.

I went to Colegio Nueva Granada which was an international school. The students were either Colombian or, for the most part, expat kids who had grown up overseas. Everybody was mellow and easy-going. During study hall, we would go to the recreation room and play really superior games of table tennis. On break sometimes kids would bring brownies laced with pot to share. It seemed like everybody in the whole country smoked pot, although that probably was not true. At lunch, we would walk to the other end of the football field to eat our sandwiches. I ate peanut butter and jelly on toast every single day for a year. Some people would bring chessboards and we would gather around and watch them play. I was at the top of my geometry class, and I think I carried about five other students through that year. Either they would copy off of my work or I would do their homework for them. I always did my homework in the five minutes between classes, and they knew that, so they would just show up early and we would do it "together."

I was on the volleyball team and got mostly A's in school. I did skip class occasionally though, probably because I could. I showed my mother my report card. Nothing below a B+ and all she said was, "What are these absences?" Oh, brother.

EL LAGO

My best friend in Bogotá was a California blonde named Holly who did not speak a word of Spanish. This was her first time out of the US. She lived about two miles from my house. At first, I took the regular bus, but I soon learned that was a bad idea. They were so crowded, I always felt hands all over me without being able to get away—I was trapped. After that I always took the minibus. These were vans that ran certain routes and cost a bit more than the bus but you got a seat and so there were no prying hands. A lot of the time I would just walk. My one rule was to get home before dark. I figured if I got home before dark, there was no reason to worry about weirdos on the street. Sometimes men would follow me, but as long as there were other people around, I did not worry about it too much.

Holly lived near a small shopping center and park area called El Lago where a lot of the "street people" hung out. These were the Colombian hippies and the American drifters who gathered to smoke pot and do deals and generally laze around and look for action. People would play frisbee and talk and eat and gather information on parties. We would go there and hang out and try to be cool.

One day it was raining (as usual) and I was standing under an archway listening to a Jesus freak proselytize and a guy appeared who had long black hair, a beret, a lavender tie-dye shirt, lavender pants and belt, and bells on his black leather boots. He walked right up to the Jesus freak, took off his hat and in a large swooping movement bowed to him and said, "And I am the Devil." This infuriated the Jesus freak and set him off on a long tirade, which was completely ignored. The Devil came up to me and asked me for a light and introduced himself as Giovanni. He was a wonderful character who loved to talk non-stop and tell stories of his escapades under the influence of magical psilocybin mushrooms—his drug of choice.

A few weeks later, Giovanni arrived dressed in a three-piece suit. I almost did not recognize him and when I questioned him he told me his grandmother had died. He had started his day with a large magical mushroom omelet and then set off for his grandmother's funeral. He went to the church all dressed up, greeted all his relatives and joined the procession to pass by and view the open casket. As he reached the casket, the mushrooms must have kicked in, because he swore to us that his grandmother moved, at which point he had apparently created a scene and was asked to leave.

Giovanni had dreams of moving to Miami to be a hairdresser or a model. When he suddenly disappeared, I wondered if he had actually made it to Miami. A few months later, I ran into his sidekick, Fernando. I had to drag it out of him, but he finally told me that Giovanni had been down in the Amazon playing "witch doctor." He was expected back soon so I told Fernando to pass a message to him to come by because I wanted to see him.

He showed up one afternoon dressed again in the three-piece suit and all his beautiful long hair cut off. I asked him who had died this time, and he was furious. Fernando apparently was supposed to have rescued all of Giovanni's clothes from his mother's house but did not get there in time, and his mother had thrown out all his lavender tie-dyes. It was obvious that at his age (somewhere in his early twenties), he was expected to get a serious job and be respectable. It was the last time I saw him, and I like to believe he become a real physician but for all I know, he is still in the jungle playing witch doctor.

It was interesting to see how many gay men lived in Colombia. Latin American men have a reputation of being super-macho. Because of Catholicism, and the taboos associated with homosexuality at the time, being gay was rarely discussed. But there were a lot of gay men in Bogotá in the '70s. Maybe it was all part of the times—the social rebellion going on around the world—or maybe there have always been a lot of Latin American homosexuals. I never saw any antagonism against them within the community at El Lago. Nobody ever really talked about it either way even though it was pretty obvious who was straight and who was not.

El Lago attracted people who indulged in drugs, and from time to time the police would show up with paddy wagons and round everybody up and take them away. One day my friend Holly got caught in one of the raids and found herself behind bars. She was not one to accept things easily and she demanded to see the person in charge. She screamed and screamed (in English) until she was taken to see "El Jefe." She told him, through another friend of ours who was acting as interpreter, that she was from the American Embassy and if he did not let her go immediately, he would have an international incident on his hands because she was not guilty of anything. (Actually, she was not, she was just in the wrong place at the wrong time.)

She told him to call the American Embassy immediately and ask them if he did not believe her. After some tense moments, when it looked like he might call her bluff, he finally let her and her interpreter friend go. Of course, once they got out, they discovered they were in a part of town they didn't know; they had no money and no way of getting home so they had to call her father and get him to come pick them up, which kind of put a damper on things. She escaped the Colombian police but did not escape parental wrath.

I met Cangrejo (the Crab) one afternoon when I was on my way home to study for an exam. I was with a couple of other friends, and he walked right up to me and asked me what my sign was. I told him "Leo" and he immediately asked me to go to a party with him. He wanted me to go downtown to the shop he owned in La Calle (which was another neighborhood closer to the center of Bogotá). He said there was a disco we could go to. This was at three in the afternoon and

I told him I thought it was a little early to be going to discos. When I said I really had to leave, he insisted I meet him the next weekend. I agreed and left. They called him Cangrejo because his face was kind of smushed like a crab, but his real name was Miguel Angel (Michelangelo). He had a real presence and was obviously not used to people saying no to him. I never did go to La Calle with him, but we became good friends. Nobody ever messed with him, so I always felt safe when he was around.

Some of the boys from school were in a band and one night they played out in the countryside and Holly and I went to hang out. A lot of people showed up and there were cars piled up all along the dirt road that led to the highway. The music was good and loud, and it was a nice evening. As the night wore on, I was sitting outside surveying the area trying to find somebody I knew to give me a ride home. My eyes landed on a familiar site: the communal pick-up truck from El Lago. I do not know who owned it, but it always seemed to appear when people were going places. I recognized the driver, Julio, and he said he would give me a ride home.

When we headed home, there were so many people in the back of the pick-up that we were scraping bottom and everybody was so messed up, they were screaming and laughing every time we hit a pothole. When the cops pulled us over, I thought we were finished for sure because half of them did not have their military ID cards and they could get arrested right away just for that.

In Colombia, one year of military service was mandatory, although a card could be purchased showing completion of service. The card was expensive and not everybody could afford it. Julio was in a panic, but we managed to sweet talk our way out of danger and the cop waved us on—only telling us to quiet down.

People from the US, England, or Venezuela would drift in and out of El Lago. One fellow from England wore only green and we called him Limey. There was an African American guy who had lived there for a long time with a Colombian woman. He was famous around town and known just as "Blackie." The rumor was that he killed his wife. I never quite believed it, but he was a bit strange.

That year Holly and I discovered Carole King's *Tapestry* album and Crosby Stills and Nash's *Déjà Vu*. We sang along to Paul Simon's "Me and Julio Down by the Schoolyard." We sat in her kitchen and ate chocolate chip cookies and washed them down with milk. At night we snuck out to attend *rumbas*, the all-night parties that were so popular in those days. We made out with guys in movie theaters. I went to see Joe Cocker's "Mad Dogs and Englishmen" tour film and could not believe how strange he was. We saw other movies that really affected us emotionally like *Billy Jack* and *Play Misty for Me*, which scared me to death. And, of course, *Shaft* was the coolest. I used to buy cigarettes from the street vendors who sold them individually, so I never had to buy a whole pack. I guess we were pretty "out there" fifteen-year-olds, but we had a lot of fun. I want to say those were more innocent times, but maybe I was just lucky and never got into anything I could not handle.

In retrospect we were hanging out with some unsavory characters who could have easily taken advantage of us. We were pretty savvy and usually did not venture out alone and tried not to go to areas we were not familiar with, but anything could have happened. Some of the guys, like "Blackie" for example, could act kind of nuts especially if they were all coked up. I never got into coke but I knew a lot of people who did.

ON TO AFRICA

After only one year, my family was on the move again. I cried on the plane all the way from Bogotá to Miami. I was not ready to leave; a year just was not long enough. Now, not only was I moving to a new place with new people, but I would have to adjust to a whole new continent and culture—plus I was going back to boarding school.

Being upset and crying when leaving a place makes me sound whiney to some people. Poor me, I was leaving South America to go to Europe and Africa. What was there to complain about? I grew up in exotic places and had all kinds of interesting experiences. People tend to think children are very adaptable and resilient. So, the combination of new adventures and the ability to constantly adapt to them must be fabulous, no?

Constantly saying goodbye to friends is not all that easy. I had to learn to compartmentalize things. I had to live in the present and tell myself: I can't think about last year. I have to focus on this year. These people, this place, this culture, this language. And so, a lot of the time things never got resolved. The grief of leaving people and places and things behind was never addressed. It just sat there in the background.

I have read a lot about people who grew up moving around frequently. Grief is a common subject. There are whole books written about dealing with the grief involved. But rarely does anybody talk about guilt. This is something I struggled with growing up. Our situation was not as privileged as some, but we were very comfortable and as I grew older and saw more of the world, I saw a big discrepancy.

Why did I live in a big house with servants and plenty to eat and a nice car and money to travel when people were living on the street in squalor and begging? I encountered beggars my whole life. Old women, children, lepers, young mothers, old men, the lame, hungry, sick, dirty, those dressed in rags or without clothes. Intellectually I came to understand that was the way of the world but the only way I could cope with it was to suppress it. I would try to block it out because I did not want to think about it. It was such an emotional thing for me, I actually made an effort not to think about it. I could not change the world. I could not do anything about it. Could I?

When my parents first started out on their grand overseas adventure, they believed they were going to change the world. They came across the same discrepancies I did and struggled to come to terms with them. At first, they thought they could change things. After a while they came to realize it was not realistic. But what they could do was help one person, or two, or three. And in doing so, they might make a small difference.

So the lesson I learned was to not judge people, to be kind and open to people, and to respect all people, no matter who they were. Everybody deserved to be listened to, whether I agreed with them or not. Everybody had worth. Well, maybe not psychopaths and mass murderers but everybody else. There were a lot of things I did not understand but I tried to be open to learning and listening. And if I could help, I tried to. But I still carried my guilt with me always. I think dealing with things like grief and guilt are a part of life. It's a process. These feelings walk alongside me but never leave me.

Sometimes I think it seems that children are super adaptable because they are better at playing make believe than grown-ups are. Sometimes I think that is why it is so hard for people like me to grow up. We get too good at playing make believe. We pretend everything is okay even if it is not.

Within months I was at a new school reinventing myself once again, but first, Africa.

PART THREE

LAGOS, NIGERIA 1972

In 1972 my father took on the job of Ford Foundation Representative for West and Central Africa which covered fifteen African countries. This included former colonies of Britain, France, and Belgium. The education and legal systems and languages were different. The main office was in Lagos, Nigeria, a place just emerging from the Biafran Civil War. The war had left many scars, physically and ethnically.

Lagos was nothing like El Lago. The whole city had a stench about it of unwashed people who were hot and sweaty all the time. Piled up garbage rotted by the side of the road and mingled with the overwhelming smell of open sewers and dead fish and rotting food.

The heat was a stifling, humid kind that takes your breath away. Everybody was dripping with sweat and clothes stuck to you. T-shirts were for wiping off sweat from your forehead. We would play tennis at seven in the morning to "avoid the heat." Never mind—we were sopping wet before we even started. Lagos is four degrees north of the equator and the climate is tropical, hot, and humid. The sun rises at 6:30 AM and sets at 6:30 PM every single day of the year.

Driving through the streets of Lagos, we passed through living room after living room, bedroom after bedroom. People lived their lives on the side of the road. Music pumped out, loud, monotonous songs that went on and on like Highlife, Afro pop, and reggae. The sounds of bumping, grinding, bouncing, boom-boom, and people dancing and singing. And the horns! Cars honked constantly. Honk,

honk, honk, honk. It did not help anything and just made noise. Maybe it made the honker feel important, but to me it was laughable. Honk, honk. Competing with the music and the sound of people yelling at each other, having disagreements or just greeting each other in loud and boisterous voices, laughing and smiling. Goats running in and out of traffic. All of this went on in the ever-present, oppressive heat. Naked children played in the open sewer. Women were having their hair done. You could buy anything from detergent to fresh fruit displayed in piles for sale. It all happened right there on the street.

Women wrapped themselves in brightly colored prints and wore elaborate head wraps or had their hair in complex wired or braided hairdos. Some of them would have a baby tied to their back with a piece of more of the same colorful cloth. They could balance anything on their head. They would run across the street in and out of traffic balancing goods on their heads and children on their backs.

There was a big sign as you came into Lagos from the airport. It said: "Welcome to Lagos." We always laughed about it because sometimes you could barely see the sign for all the piles of garbage heaped up around it. The roads were mostly paved, but the sides were all dirt, dust, and piles of garbage. I imagined that at some point somebody must pick up garbage, but they could not keep up with it. It was always there in piles along the side of the road. And it stank of rotting food. I almost expected to see dead bodies in there. I often saw big rats roaming about. That combined with the open sewers and the unwashed bodies in high heat made the smell overpowering.

The interesting thing was that as much as the smell hit you when you first arrived, after you had been there a few weeks, you actually got used to it. You did not notice the smell and it became normal. Your brain banished it to some forgotten place. But if you left and came back, there it was again—until you got used to it again. Sometimes I wondered if the Nigerians disliked the sanitized, perfumed smells of Europe and the US—or if they noticed it.

During my first week in Lagos, we went to the airport to see some people off at night. As we were driving through the dark streets, I made out a figure of a naked man with matted hair, hopping along from garbage pile to garbage pile with a crazed look in his eyes. He would pick things out of the garbage and eat them and hop to the next pile without caring about being naked. I had seen poverty and dirty living conditions in Latin America, but they did not approach that of Lagos. Everything was so different and it was hard to take it all in. On top of that, people were always trying to touch me. The lepers who begged outside the grocery store would reach out to me. Children would try to touch my white skin or my soft straight hair. I was a teenager so it gave me the creeps. My first summer in Lagos, I dreaded leaving the house.

Lagos was a big business center and an important place to be on the West African coast. It was booming with oil money. People were packed into every available space and the traffic was not to be believed. It could take three hours just to go from our house to the airport, which was about fifteen miles away.

The city sat on three islands and a strip of mainland. The islands were mainly occupied by government buildings, diplomat and expat residences, museums, and hotels. The mainland was the business center with offices and shops and suburbia spread out from there. This wreaked havoc with traffic because if one of the bridges was clogged (which happened daily!) cars would sit for hours waiting to move. Everybody made a habit of carrying a book with them whenever they went anywhere by car in preparation for a "go slow."

There were signs all over the city that said: "No urinating here," but people paid little attention. Since most people did not have access to plumbing or toilets, they would either pay for public toilets or use a ditch for free. Often the public pay toilet was just an empty lot that somebody patrolled, selling a piece of old newspaper and a spot to relieve yourself.

We lived in a big house on Ikoyi Island right on the bay (though the bay no longer exists because they filled it in to build a highway). It was a perfect tropical house because three sides were all windows which, when opened, would catch the breezes. The front and back section was all screened-in, but the side panel was not. We rarely opened it because of the mosquitoes but one night it was so hot we decided to chance it. We were gazing out and admiring the tree that ran along the side of the house when we saw a huge rat crawling along toward the opened window. We decided to suffer the heat after that.

We had rats inside the house, too. The cook was always putting traps out for them and he often caught them. Once, when I knew there was one around and the traps had been set, I got up in the morning and went to put on my leather sandals. Somebody or something had taken a huge bite out of one of the leather straps—it had teeth marks on it! I took it down to the cook and showed it to him. I was freaked out; it not only meant that my sandals were ruined, but also that a rat (and they were always giant rats in Lagos) had actually been in my room upstairs. *Yuck!* The cook, Philip, laughed and laughed. Apparently it was the funniest thing he had seen in a long time.

LIFE IN LAGOS

One thing I noticed right away in Lagos was the way people greeted you. When you arrived home or at somebody's house, you were always greeted with, "Welcome" or "You are Welcome." I loved that and incorporated it into my culture and I try to use it to this day.

It was a challenge for anybody to survive day-to-day in Lagos. The population at the time was 1.5 million. (Today it's 16.5 million.) Besides the traffic, heat, overpopulation, and overall hustle and bustle, there were problems with water, electricity, and telephones. It could take a week to place a call to the US, if you were lucky. The electricity used to go off for days at a time—usually when my mother was planning a dinner party. Many times, the reason for an electrical blackout resulted from somebody hitting the utility pole with their car. Basically anybody there could easily get a driver's license and they all drove like maniacs with no regard for traffic rules or people.

My mother wrote to her sister-in-law:

February 1973

As I sit here writing this, our electricity has been out for 10.5 hours with no sign of it ever returning, and we are having 25 people in for a cocktail party tonight (with ice, deviled eggs, shrimp, etc. in the refrigerator slowly getting warm and probably spoiled). The weather is around 90 degrees and the humidity should be the same! It is not just our isolated neighborhood but our whole island is having trouble, and probably other areas also.

We are not only living in a developing country in West Africa but we are also living in a city plagued by unbelievable population growth in the past 10 years. This, coupled with affluence (from oil money), which means many new automobiles and motorcycles, shortages of services of all kinds, and congestion beyond imagination. Bill leaves the house at 7:15 each morning in order to beat the traffic. He can get to the office in 10 minutes going that early, whereas if he waits until 7:30 it will take him 45 minutes and he often will get out and walk the last 7 or 8 blocks and lets the driver sit in the traffic.

We are a typical tropical climate with palm trees, lovely flowers, lizards, bugs, rats, filth of all kinds, mildew within a few days on everything. This used to be called the coast of the "White Man's Grave" because of malaria, and we all take malaria depressants either weekly or daily. We also are careful to keep up our cholera shots.

It is amazing the number of people who find their way to Lagos, for one reason or another. A few days ago, I was astounded to see Bill bringing home two elderly ladies for tea. One lives in a retirement home in Whitewater, Wisconsin, where my mother lives and of course knows her. They are on a world tour (23 retired teachers) and my mother, Fern, told them "Call on Virginia" and they did. We had a nice visit and Bill talked to the group for about half an hour the next morning.

We have four servants. A very good cook who also cleans the downstairs and sort of runs the household and the compound. A steward who is sweet, simple and honest who does the laundry, serves the table and drinks and is in charge of upstairs. A gardener who works every day, all day, except the weekends. And a night watchman who is here from six to six each night. This is pretty standard. These houses, being so open and not very well made, are rather difficult to keep clean and to keep bugs and animals out. Everything in the kitchen that would attract anything must be kept in the refrigerator, freezer, or in tight containers. We still fight these tiny ants constantly although I cannot figure out what attracts them. We sometimes have them in the living room and they BITE.

Food in Lagos is mostly imported and is very expensive. We can shop in a clean, attractive Swiss Supermarket with all the Swiss cheeses and chocolates along with many other luxuries and very good meat. We can also shop in a French supermarket with perfumes, fancy liquors, and also good meat. And there is an English supermarket, which has the same things as the others but is not nearly as imaginative nor luxurious. There are also Lebanese and Syrian supermarkets. These markets are chains which are all over West Africa. We buy our fresh vegetables and fruits at the open market, and baking soda at the pharmacy. Foremost Dairies provides milk products—it is reconstituted in Nigeria and provides cottage cheese, ice cream, and milk.

Lagos does not offer much in the way of entertainment and there are very few really good restaurants. There are almost no good movies and nightclubs are interesting but for most people as a one-time-only sort of thing. There is a national museum lecture or program once a month and a concert about every three months, so mostly people fend for themselves.

Having servants does not mean that one simply turns the whole operation over and lives a life of luxury. I do most of the shopping, plan the meals, and have to constantly oversee the kitchen and house even though my cook is intelligent and very good. I learned a long time ago that if you want things to go right you must oversee the operation yourself.

Love, Virginia

Our cook, Phillip, was from Cameroon and spoke French. He had learned to cook in the army and was considered to be one of the best cooks in Lagos. He made the most delicious coq au vin I ever tasted. My mother freaked out when she saw him put butter in the pan to cook bacon, but it sure tasted good. He made crepes instead of pancakes, which I much preferred, and we always had yummy pastry treats with afternoon tea.

Phillip did most of the shopping for food in the open market. There were a couple of grocery stores where my mother shopped that carried imported goods although the supply was erratic. You could usually find caviar and sardines, but it was rare to see flour. My mother, however, loved to go to the open market to buy cloth and beads and I would go with her from time to time, which was always an experience. The women who ran the market were very large, confident businesswomen. In this part of the country, they were mostly of the Yoruba tribe. The Yoruba women ran businesses up and down the West African coast. When the bargaining started there would always be a dramatic display. They would quote you a price and you would cut it in half and one of them would fall back in a faint and another one would catch her. When they had recovered from the initial "shock," negotiations would begin. I'm sure they *always* got a good deal.

One time when I was at the market I started wandering around and came upon a stall that had something hanging above it that I couldn't quite identify at first. It looked like it was moving yet it wasn't. It finally dawned on me that it was a horse's head with maggots crawling all over it like a river. I looked down to the counter to see what other things were on display. After recognizing various other animal parts I realized it was a juju stall. They had everything for the witch doctor's needs—all very creepy.

In the summer I would get together with friends from boarding school and we would take a banana boat out to one of the beaches. The boat's gunwale would sit just above water level, and I was always sure we were going to sink. We almost never went swimming since the undercurrents at the beach were so strong; they would pull you out into the ocean and you would never get back. Sometimes there was a lifeguard with a long rope who might be able to save you but mostly we just decided to sit on the beach and drink Cokes.

My parents invited a newly arrived family to our house for dinner one night. The boy was about my age and seemed sad. He had recently lost his mother. So, I was nice to him and later that summer I invited him to come to the beach with us. When we got out to the beach, he dove in and started swimming out away from shore. None of us could believe our eyes. We kept yelling at him to come back in because we thought he would drown for sure. We could see he was struggling but he did manage to swim along the shore and make it back to land. Afterwards everybody was wondering why he did that. A few days later he showed up at my house and apologized for being such an ass. Apparently, he thought he could impress me with his actions since he had taken a liking to me. Quite the opposite effect occurred.

I never liked Lagos much and used to count the days until I could go back to school. It was very difficult to get around and socialize on my own. Everything had to be planned, and drivers had to be arranged.

We lived on the island of Ikoyi and belonged to the Ikoyi Club. It had a swimming pool, tennis courts, and a dining room. On Sunday nights they showed old movies on an outdoor screen which was the main form of entertainment. Most of my friends lived on a different island so I did not see them often. Life for me was kind of boring, although I did read a lot of books.

BACK TO BOARDING SCHOOL, LUGANO, SWITZERLAND

Many children of parents who lived abroad did stints in boarding schools. Reasons for expat kids going to boarding schools ranged from parents living in places where there were no schools, to parents who wanted to park their kids while they went off and did their own thing, and everything in between. My mother started out home schooling my brothers in Pyinmana because there was no school up country but after I was born, it became difficult for my mother to juggle caring for me and teaching them. She wrote:

January 27, 1957

Bill spent the afternoon writing letters about getting the boys into a boarding school in India. We have decided that would be the best thing for them since I just can't do a good job teaching with Kathleen in my arms, and then too the boys need more competition, organized recreations, coeducation, etc. They are not doing their best work by far for me. We are applying at Kodaikanal, South India (between Madras and Bangalore) because it is in the low mountains and almost purely an American school. The other possibility is Woodstock up in the Himalayas in Mussoorie. I'm afraid the climate might stir up Tim's respiratory troubles up there, although maybe not. Both are schools for missionary's children primarily and kept up to standard with the schools at home so that high school graduates may go right into most colleges.

My brothers went to India when they were nine and eleven. I always thought that that was very young to go to boarding school, but I later found out there were children as young as six at that same school. They spent two years in India and a year in the Philippines. When my oldest brother went off to college the other brother went to boarding school in the US. I started boarding school at thirteen and lived at home only one year after that, when I was fifteen. In those days there was no email or even phones in lots of cases. Once you were dropped off at school, that was it. You saw your parents once or twice a year and were lucky to get mail. My brother went to one boarding school where he could not get breakfast on Sunday unless he turned in a letter to his parents. My mother often received a blank page in the mail. She would say, "At least I know he's alive."

At boarding school friends became family and we came to rely on each other. There was a bond that I made with my high school boarding school friends that never has been broken. They are to this day my global family.

My parents sent us mainly so we would get a better education. My mother wrote diligently so I often had letters in my mailbox. The only time I was ever homesick was at school in Texas when I was very sick with the flu and was coughing at night. The dorm counselor told me to shut up. I just wanted my mom. My brother fared worse however; he got the mumps at the end of the school year and could not go home until he got over it.

When we moved to Nigeria, it was decided I would go to school in Switzerland. It ended up being a much more pleasant experience than Texas had been. The American School in Switzerland (TASIS) had a campus in the mountains above Lake Lugano, in the Italian part of Switzerland. The main building was called De Nobili and had been designated a historical landmark. It housed administrative offices, the salon, the dining room, and the girls' housing on the upper floors. This was surrounded by a couple of prefab buildings and rented houses in the community for additional living areas. Another large villa was across the street where the library and theater were on the lower levels and the boys were housed on the upper levels. Most of the classrooms were in prefab buildings. The gym, for instance, was a bubble-like structure. Ultimately the school was a work in progress. The founder Mary Christ Fleming (or Mama Fleming) had a vision and was always raising money to realize it. She had started the school in the mid-fifties with 10 children, and there were 200 by the time I graduated in 1974. It was a little rustic but very homey and we felt like one large family. Today it is a very expensive, upscale school with large modern villas instead of the prefab buildings.

At TASIS, there were not many rules. We had times when we were supposed to be in our dorms and times when the lights were supposed to be out, but things were flexible. We did not have to sign out if we wanted to go on a hike or into town. Our free time was basically our own, and we had a lot of it. We could explore the Swiss countryside and the small villages that surrounded us. A frequent haunt for students was the overgrown garden outside the building where the writer Heman Hesse had lived. It was on a winding pathway up to the small town of Montagnola. We often spent weekend evenings at a place we called the Hole in the Wall where an old woman served beverages and snacks out of her own kitchen.

We were encouraged to be independent and learn from our surroundings. We could smoke and drink in moderation with parental permission, which my parents granted me knowing I was a hopeless case and would just do it anyway. Most of the teachers were young and enjoyed what they were doing. They got to know us as people and showed us respect; in turn we got to know and respect them. It was a completely different atmosphere than Texas. I felt like I could breathe there.

We spent the two weeks after Christmas in St. Moritz skiing. We had classes in the mornings and then we skied in the afternoon. We stayed in a big modern hotel for tourists. Some of the rooms could fit as many as ten or twelve people in them. I could sit at my window and watch the horse races on the frozen lake below. There was a picturesque little town where we could eat raclette and other delicious cheesy things. Yes, it was school, but really it was an immersion in culture and life.

There were things about boarding school that were not good, of course. The food was generally bad. In Lugano we had mystery meat most nights and anchovy pizza on Fridays. The croissants for breakfast on the weekends were left outside the kitchen early in the morning so most of them were gone by the time they got set out in the dining room. You had to be an early bird to catch a fresh one. You did not choose whom you lived with and were lucky if you liked your roommate. There was no TV and you had to listen to everybody else's music at all hours. I had one roommate who fell asleep to Yes's *Close to the Edge* album every single night, which drove me nuts. My bed was next to the door and another roommate of mine could never quite manage to close the door on her way out. Because of this, I would freeze in the winter.

There was one phone for all the students located in the main building. Somebody was assigned to stay by the phone every evening so that if a call came in, the person watching the phone would run all over campus looking for the person who was being called. It could take a while to locate them, and you had to hope the line had not been disconnected in the meantime. My parents would usually send me a letter or a cable telling me when they were going to call so I could sit by the phone waiting—if I got the letter in time, that is. People usually didn't bother to call unless it was really important.

During my junior year my boyfriend and I were pretty serious about each other. We spent a lot of time together hiking and exploring the countryside. I consensually lost my virginity that year. It was funny because a lot of my girlfriends had been insinuating all year that they were not virgins but after I lost mine, I found out they were all making it up to sound cool. It kind of made me feel stupid—but ultimately I did not regret it. It was a positive experience. My boyfriend was a year older, so he graduated and was gone by my senior year.

In truth, I had been groped and propositioned by men most of my life. I had been followed and chased in Mexico, groped by drunks on airplanes, groped by men on crowded subways and buses, grabbed at on the streets of Rome, propositioned on airplanes and in airports. One man on an airplane told me he would buy me anything I wanted—furs, diamonds—if I would spend the afternoon with him, no strings attached. I could not help but laugh in his face. In Latin America, I figured it was the culture that made the men prey on me and harass me. But when I moved to Africa, the men were the same. They were the same the world over. It made me feel self-conscious. I was a friendly person, but I learned to avoid talking to random men who approached me. I learned I did not want anything to do with them. When I was growing up as a teenager I always felt like an object.

My senior year at boarding school I spent time in the library studying in the evenings and I always sat with the same two boys. We were friends and we laughed a lot together. One of them always needed help with his French homework, and the other one was just a joker. One night I was walking back to my dorm from the library with the joker. We were in a fairly secluded area, and he pushed me onto the ground and held me down and started to take my clothes off. He was a big guy. Breathing on me he said, "Go ahead, scream all you like. Nobody can hear you." Scream? What? Yes, I should have screamed, but nothing came out. I could not make a sound or move—I was frozen. And he proceeded to rape me. I tried to think about anything else and to pretend I was not there. Let him do his deed and let me out of here. I just wanted it to be over. Afterwards, he got up and walked away without saying a word. I went back to my dorm fuming but I did not tell anybody because I knew it was my word against his. And he would never admit it. I knew I was powerless. Those were the days when people mostly thought women provoked the men into doing things like that. Or people just did not want to talk about it.

At the time, my roommate knew something was wrong, but we did not discuss it until ten years later. She agreed that telling people would not have done me any good. I tried to avoid him for the rest of the year, but I have run into him at reunions over the years and at one point I confronted him about it. He acted shocked, like he had no idea what I was talking about. A complete jerk. An apology would have been the least he could do. The fact that I thought he was a good friend of mine made it much worse. Could I not trust anybody? I really hated the power men had (and still have) over women.

I learned at a very young age that bad things happen, but you always have to keep going. Plane crashes do not keep you from traveling, moving does not stop you from making new friends, and bad experiences at school do not stop you from going to school. The memories got shelved. I just had to pick myself up and move on.

Looking back at my time in boarding school, I certainly could have done much worse. I took a poll of my friends who went to boarding school and asked them what their biggest challenge was. Most of them said, "Saying goodbye to friends." One said, "I have left many places but only cried for one." When I left TASIS, it was difficult to say goodbye to my friends but this time most of them were also moving on to new places, different colleges around the US or Europe, so we were all in the same boat.

My time at that school also formed part of my culture. I had been maneuvering airports on my own for a while but in Europe, I had to be mindful of train and bus schedules. I planned my own trips, places to stay, things to see, and figured out how to get around on subways. I was also heavily influenced by the overwhelming beauty of Lugano. I had grown up in the mountains of Mexico and Colombia, but the Alps took mountains to another level. And the sight of mountains and lakes combined was ... I have no words. Waking up to that view every morning was almost like a religious experience—calming and friendly. It made me feel optimistic, that life was worth living. We would hike straight up the mountains through the woods and come out into big lush meadows and roll in the grass. I had always enjoyed being in nature but this sealed the deal for me. It became a part of me. Give me a lake and a mountain and I am happy.

SNAPSHOTS FROM EUROPE

IN-PROGRAM TRAVEL

We had three In-Program Travels during the year. That meant we all went on a four-day weekend to someplace in Europe and were expected to drink up the culture and see a lot of museums and important sites. Sometimes we would have to write a report on it. I took a course in art history, and we went to Ravenna, Italy and wrote about the mosaics and after a trip to Florence, Italy we wrote about the paintings. Other trips I took were to Venice, Munich, and Dachau, one of the Nazi concentration camps. Dachau was an eerie place, and we were all greatly moved by it. In Munich we ate at McDonald's because it was so weird to see a McDonald's in Germany. We also sang along to the oompah-pah bands at the Hofbrauhaus, a famous German beer hall. In Venice we got around on water buses and discovered a small disco. However at one point a pigeon landed on my head in St. Mark's Square. And I hate pigeons. The canals were dirty and smelly. Venice was not one of my favorites

GREECE

Besides the required school trips, there were other trips available during spring break and Christmas break. In the springtime, students could choose between Russia and Greece. I went to Greece and the chaperones were the art history teacher and her husband, an English teacher. We toured Athens and the southern peninsula, stopping in Olympia and Delphi. Then we got on a small cruise ship and toured the islands of Mykonos, Rhodes, and Crete.

Our cabins were in the bowels of the ship and we could see half water and half sky out of our portholes. The boys spent most of their time having spit wad wars and terrorizing the girls. The dining room was cordoned off, so we (the horrible teenage horde) were not visible to the rest of the travelers. We ate so much we would practically roll back to our cabins at night. Greece was someplace I had always dreamed of going to since I was fascinated by the history. I was not disappointed. Although almost everything we saw was in ruins, it was still exciting to soak it all in. In Olympia, we spent an evening in a restaurant where we had a great time learning traditional dances and drinking ouzo. It made for a well-rounded education.

ITALY

I also went to Florence twice. Once just for fun and once with my art history class. On one trip I got caught up in a group that was climbing up to the dome of the cathedral, il Duomo. I did not realize what I was getting myself into until I was herded out onto this narrow wooden railing that went all the way around the inside of the base of the dome. Now we're talking about being quite high up off the ground. This was the first time I discovered I had severe vertigo. I tried to go back the way I came but there were too many people so I started to panic and was about to cry when a friend of mine grabbed my hand and led me around to the other side where we could go outside and sit to see a view of the city. We sat there and smoked cigarettes until I calmed down and then he led me back. You can still climb up to the dome, but the railing around the dome is much sturdier than it used to be.

I traipsed around northern Italy and saw places like Giotto's Chapel and the large square in Siena where horse races are held twice a year. We were impressed by the fact that it was the location where the 1968 film *Romeo and Juliet* was filmed. However, we were there to see the mosaics in the Siena cathedral.

PARIS

A friend of mine from my grade school days in Mexico was living in Paris so one November I headed there for a long weekend. It was my first trip to Paris and it snowed lightly the whole time I was there. My friend, Lisa, was in school and her mother insisted I take a bus tour of the city to get an overview. After that I was on my own. I was sixteen. There were two things I wanted to see; one was Notre Dame and the other was the Louvre. I found Notre Dame with no problem. I walked into the empty building. It was dark and took me a while to get my eyes used to it. It was quiet and peaceful. I made my way down towards the apse and as I reached it, light flooded in. I looked up and saw the most beautiful rosette-stained glass windows I had ever seen. I sat down and meditated on them for a while.

From there I headed to the Louvre. It took me a while to find it and the entrance did not seem to be very clearly marked but I did manage to buy a ticket and start my tour. I did not have much time, so I decided to just see three things and then leave. I found *Winged Victory* and the *Venus de Milo* right away, but I could not find the *Mona Lisa*. I walked up and down an entire wing of paintings. I saw painters set up with their easels copying the famous artworks, something I had never seen before in a museum. There was lots of great art, but no *Mona Lisa*. I wandered into a room that was full of old jewelry. No sign of her there. I was just about to give up and leave when I happened upon a small room off to the side that had a lot of paintings all hung up together on one of the walls. I was looking at these various, random paintings when right in the middle of them, the *Mona Lisa* jumped out at me. I could not believe it. I stood there, transfixed.

It was a magical day. I have been back to Paris many times, but Notre Dame has always been very crowded and stifling. The Louvre now has a grand entrance and signs all over the place directing you to the Mona Lisa, which has such a big protective case that you can barely see it. I was very lucky to have seen it up close.

ROME

Since my friend, Patti, had grown up in Rome, she and I spent a long weekend visiting her old stomping grounds. One of the highlights was the chocolate gelato on the Via Veneto. No place makes ice cream like Italy. We were there not long after a crazy guy had attacked the Pietà in St. Peter's Basilica with a hammer and it had been restored. I was glad it was back and we could see it but now there was a thick pane of glass in front of it. I knew it was marble but it looked like porcelain. From there we wandered through the Vatican Museum and the Sistine Chapel. They were restoring the chapel so there was scaffolding all through it but in a way it was nicer that way because there were very few people.

In those days, travel in Europe was much less complicated and society was just more open in general; from time to time we did, however, run across anti-American sentiments and would often tell people we were Canadian in these situations. As teens travelling alone, we also had to develop a really good "creep radar" so we could tell who we could trust and who we could not.

CALIFORNIA 1974

> *"Reentry is a significant event for the Absentee American; the experience may be vividly recollected decades later. Respondents described reentry as difficult, painful, turbulent, or traumatic... The experience is often referred to as a shock. In professional literature on the subject, this transition is generally referred to as euphoria, irritability, hostility, gradual adjustment, and adaptation."*
>
> –Carolyn D. Smith, The Absentee American

After graduating from TASIS, I enrolled at Mills College in Oakland, California. I had no idea where to go to school in the US, but I applied to schools in Minnesota, Ohio, and California. My friends told me I belonged in California—although of course none of them had been there. They just thought that's where all the crazy, fun people were. I decided to go to California because it was relatively warm and I knew people who would be in the general area. Also, since it was a women's college, I thought I might learn more about women and women's issues and it would help me to develop that side of myself.

My first year was very difficult. I did not know it then, but I was experiencing reverse culture shock. Today there are resources to help people returning to their passport country adapt to life there. There are now also books on how to transition to college and courses on what to expect. I had none of that. I was in a place that was foreign to me and was experiencing college for the first time, too. I had real trouble figuring things out. I wondered: What was wrong with me? Why could I not fit in?

I arrived in California after spending the previous two years in Europe where it was considered the norm to travel and have wine and beer with a meal. I knew nothing about American pop culture. The girls I met had gone to American high schools where cheerleading, proms, and staying out late sneaking beer were the highlights. They loved to tell stories about what they did in high school. So, I told stories, too. These girls did not like my stories and a few of them told people that I was bragging, or sometimes even that I was lying. It got to the point where if I started to talk, people would turn away or ignore me. I did not understand why, and I thought there was something wrong with me. I had never had a problem fitting in before, but I could not identify with these people at all and they could not identify with me either. The thing was, I looked and talked like them, but really I was a foreigner. It was a very lonely time for me.

My friends from high school had to adjust to being back in the US, too. One friend told me a funny story. She and another friend of ours went to college in Colorado. After moving in and getting settled they decided to go have some wine. They went into a bar and ordered two glasses and were asked for their IDs. They showed them and were told they could not be served because they were underage. My friend did not understand. What did they mean? She had no idea there was such a thing as a drinking age. We were all out of our element.

I was very naive and had no understanding of the racial problems that still existed in the US. I had been in multicultural, international environments my entire life. I knew there were bigoted people in the world, but I hadn't encountered any firsthand. One day I went to lunch in the school cafeteria, and I saw a long empty table and I thought: I'll sit there and then maybe I'll meet some new people. The place was filling up and I figured that people were bound to sit there. Also, it was in a different part of the cafeteria than where I usually sat so I figured maybe I would meet different kinds of girls—they could not all be strange and nasty. Well, as lunch progressed people did sit around me; they were all Black and none of them would speak to me, not even to say "hello." The next day I commented on it to somebody, and they told me whites were not allowed to sit at that table—it was for the Black girls only. Apparently Black and white girls did not mix. It was too bad, because surely these Black girls had had different experiences than me, and I probably could have learned some things from them about their perspective of America.

My first experience meeting Black Americans made me very confused. I did not understand why they were so angry at me. I had not even known there was segregation in the United States as recently as the 1960s and frankly I was pretty shocked to find that out. I thought that many of the problems Black Americans had were also problems that women generally had in the US and around the world. I would have thought that in a place like Mills there would have been a lot more understanding about the common plight of all minorities including women, but it just was not like that. And I obviously did not know enough about it. Unfortunately I could not learn more about it from them. And I was having a lot of problems of my own, so I just let it be.

So, for me, I had some rude awakenings when I first arrived in the US on several levels. But at the time, it was mostly personal. I had always been able to shift, to adjust, to slip into a new place—but this was different. I could not figure it out, even though I pulled out everything I had in my toolbox. I knew I had to live in the present and persevere, but I stopped talking to people and retreated into myself. My roommate wanted to move dorms where she could have a single room. I agreed and moved to an older dorm into a small single room, where I became even more isolated. Eventually I did attend some frat parties and dated a couple of guys briefly. The people in the new dorm were a bit more friendly and I started to get to know some of them and open up again.

An old friend from TASIS showed up halfway through my freshman year and confirmed that I had not lost my mind. He assured me that the problems I was having were not because of me, it was other people, or just the situation. But that definitely nothing was wrong with me. It made me feel better but by that time my chameleon instincts had kicked in and I had learned from my initial experiences. I no longer told anybody where I was from or anything about my past. I just kept my mouth shut and went with the flow. Eventually I found a more worldly, interesting group of people and made some very close friends who I still keep in touch with, but it did take a while. And I learned to not tell my story to people right out of the gate.

In some ways Mills was like being in the womb. It sat in the middle of East Oakland, which at that time had one of the highest crime rates in America. The Mills campus was a little oasis where everything was lush and beautiful. Eucalyptus trees lined the avenues and a pleasant little stream ran through it. The dormitories were mainly made up of single rooms that shared porches. The weather was sunny and warm. And it was also peaceful because no men were around to hassle you, hustle you, or dominate in the classroom.

After some time, I welcomed life at Mills. I realized the strength and the power that we had as women and also the limitations and the problems that we were up against. I learned that there were women out there who were doing a lot and who were very successful. I was living in a time when women were coming of age and our rights were expanding. Mills was just women looking after women and I did learn a lot about what being a woman was all about.

ON SAFARI IN KENYA AND TANZANIA

On my first Christmas vacation in college, I had a memorable plane trip on my way to Africa. I was to fly from San Francisco to Minneapolis to Nairobi and meet my parents for a two-week camera safari in Kenya and Tanzania. I made my flight arrangements through a travel agent in New York and understood that I would change planes in Geneva.

I arrived in Geneva at 7 AM and went to the transit desk. They told me that I could go into town or get a room at the airport if I wanted because the flight did not leave until midnight that night and that

I was wait-listed anyway. What? I had not looked closely at the ticket. There I was in Geneva, Switzerland. I had only a $20 traveler's check to my name, and I was wait-listed on a flight that left at midnight. There was nothing I could do but wait and see. I spent all day dozing on airport seats and reading my book. I did not eat anything because I figured I should save my money and anyway, I was too nervous to eat. Finally, it came time to check in for the flight. I went to the gate, and they told me I would have to wait until everybody else had boarded the plane. I was a nervous wreck.

I kept picturing myself stranded in Geneva, eating out of the vending machines and spending Christmas by myself in the terminal. How would I let my parents know where I was? Finally, the airline called the stand-by passengers to the desk. They told me there was one seat left but I had to go downstairs and get my seat assignment. I raced down the stairs but there was nobody there. I waited a while in a panic and then I ran back up the stairs and told them there was nobody down there. A woman got up and said she would go get it for me while I went through security again. As soon as I had my seat assignment, I ran all the way across the tarmac to the plane. I was scared to death they would take off without me. When I reached my seat, I buckled my seat belt and broke into tears of relief.

I arrived in Nairobi the next morning, but there was nobody there to meet me. I went to the bank and cashed my $20 traveler's check, deciding I would have to take my chances with a taxi. I went out to the parking lot and there were lots of taxis lined up but no people around at all. While I was standing there trying to figure out what to do an airline steward came walking up and I asked him how to get a taxi. He said he did not know but it was not safe for me to go anywhere in a taxi. I knew that but what choice did I have? He asked his captain if they could give me a ride, and the captain agreed. I absolutely believe in the kindness of strangers.

An airline minibus dropped me off at the hotel. I rang my parents' room. No answer. I rang our friends' room. No answer. I walked all around the hotel lobby and outdoor area. When I returned to the lobby there was my mother sitting on the couch.

She took one look at me and said, "What are you doing here?" At this point, I was exhausted, hungry, confused, and frankly a little pissed off. "Thanks, Mom," I said. She replied calmly, not knowing my state of mind, "Your father is out at the airport looking for you." Apparently our communication had gotten really screwed up somehow and they thought I was coming in on a flight from Rome. I wish I could say this was an unfamiliar scenario, but having travelled the million miles that I have, this kind of thing happened all the time.

I soon forgot my ordeal and was excited to get on the road. Seeing the animals of East Africa had long been my dream. We headed out of town to Nairobi National Park, Tsavo National Park, and Amboseli Game Reserve in southern Kenya. Nairobi is about 120 miles south of the equator at 5,800 feet, so it was warm but not too hot. The Great Rift Valley runs through Kenya and the landscape consists of vast plains and hills with trees popping up here and there. Instead of forest, there are mostly open areas where you can see far into the distance. We stood on the equator near Nanyuki at over 6,000 feet and it was quite chilly.

In the parks we stayed in camps and slept in tents that were fairly large and had cots in them with mosquito nets and a bucket in the back for the toilet. There was a communal dining hall where everybody sat on benches and ate family style.

One day, we were driving through one park right at dusk and we came upon a lone baby zebra. The game warden was with us and he seemed upset. We asked him what the problem was and he said the zebra would be dead by dark. He said it must have been separated from the rest of the herd somehow and now it did not have a chance. We asked if maybe we could take it with us or help it in some way and of course there was nothing we could do. That was just the way things worked; the world was one big food chain. It was still heartbreaking for me to witness this fact in person.

We crossed over into Tanzania and went to Ngorongoro, a huge volcanic crater with a large plain inside where wildebeest, flamingoes, hyenas, lions, rhinos, hippos, and monkeys all co-existed. It had a very prehistoric, eerie feel to it. The only way to get to it was in a four-wheel drive Jeep that could creep over the edge of the volcanic rock that completely surrounded the area. As we were driving across the middle of the plain, we encountered a family of rhinos. Rhinos cannot see well but they hear well and have a good sense of smell. We were downwind from them, but the noise of the engine must have taken them by surprise because they turned and started to run right at us. The driver immediately turned off the engine. The rhinos froze in their tracks and we did too. Pretty soon the rhinos turned and started to walk away but then changed their minds. We sat perfectly still for about twenty minutes while the mama and papa rhino had a quickie and the baby was the lookout.

We also saw several lions that day and they were curious about us. One even climbed onto the hood of the car to have a better look at us.

Luckily, he could not get in. We also stopped along the way for a picnic near a small lake and ran around with some small monkeys. We saw some hyenas chasing flamingos along the shore. They were really ugly things, rather scary looking. And the hippos were floating in their pond.

Another day at a different park we came up behind a herd of elephants crossing the road. There was an auntie at the end and she turned and started running towards us, ears flapping and trunk trumpeting. She took our driver by surprise. He shoved the car in reverse going full speed backwards in retreat. We were all a bit shaken by the elephant's behavior. This was a very different elephant experience than I had had in Burma when I was riding on top of one. When we were a safe distance away, and the elephants had moved on a little, to my disbelief the driver went back down the same road to try again. This time when they charged us, the driver was ready for them and he gunned his engine. The elephants were afraid of the noise and backed off. When we returned to camp that day, we were told it was becoming rarer and rarer to be charged by animals because they were becoming too accustomed to people. That was good news to us but really bad news in the larger sense of things.

On the way back to Nairobi we camped at the foot of Kilimanjaro. None of us were adventurous enough to climb it but we enjoyed having it as our backdrop. From there we headed north to spend New Year's Eve at the Outspan Hotel in Nyeri, Kenya. We stopped on the way at Lake Nakuru National Park to see the thousands upon thousands of flamingoes. They would fly in a circular pattern like a cone going up into the sky.

In Aberdare National Park, not far from Nyeri, there was a place called Treetops. It was a hotel originally built in a tree located next to a famous salt lick. It burned down and was rebuilt, but as you walked along the corridors you could still see branches coming through the walls. We arrived in the afternoon and had to trek a ways to the hotel from the bus. We all had tea up on the roof. The baboons were really gutsy and came up and tried to steal some women's handbags. We had been warned about them. At night, animals came for the salt and so there was lots of activity. My friends stayed in the Queen Elizabeth suite, named so because the queen-to-be had been staying there when her father, George the VI, died in 1952.

Even though I have such good memories of that trip, I have no desire to go back; I'm not sure I would like to see how much everything has changed.

IBADAN, NIGERIA

After living in Lagos for three years, my father retired from the Ford Foundation and took a job as the Director General of the International Institute of Tropical Agriculture (IITA) in Ibadan, Nigeria, eighty miles north of Lagos.

Life in Ibadan was quite different because we did not actually live in Ibadan itself but about ten miles out of town on a large agricultural research farm. On the farm scientists worked on crop development and easing world hunger as part of the Green Revolution, which had begun in the 1960s. In 1975, IITA was one of eight research institutes around the world. These eight institutes were each working on a specific crop or policy approach: tropical agriculture (Nigeria and Colombia), rice (the Philippines), potatoes (Peru), livestock (Ethiopia), semi-arid tropics (India), and food policy (USA). The first institute built was CYMMIT (the International Maize and Wheat Improvement Center) in Mexico where Norm Borlaug worked on wheat for which he received the Nobel Peace Prize in 1970. He and my father were both from Iowa and they knew each other pretty well. Since 1975, institutes for forestry research, water management, and aquatic resource management have been added.

All of the institutes fall under the CGIAR (Consultative Group for International Agricultural Research) umbrella. Their work continues today. "CGIAR is a global research partnership for a food-secure future dedicated to transforming food, land, and water systems in a climate crisis." They have expanded their focus and are now involved in many new initiatives including gender equality and environmental health.

Each institute worked on foods that the people in the area raised—for West Africa it was roots and tubers (yams, cassava), rice, legumes, and field corn. They also worked on farming systems and storage buildings using resources that were readily available to the average African farmer. They had large controlled fields on the compound and some sites out in the countryside to test different seeds in a more hostile environment.

The compound itself was an artificial environment because it was pretty much self-contained and always very clean. There were no stinky smells of sewers or garbage heaps. The grounds were manicured, the streets were in good repair, and the buildings were modern with central air-conditioning. We had our own lake and a water treatment plant so we could drink the water out of the tap. We had our own generators so if the electricity went out, the labs would still function. We had our own club with a pool, a golf course, a snack bar and guest rooms. There was also a large Conference and Training Center and a decent cafeteria.

There were always people coming in to take short- and long-term courses. These people mainly came from around Africa and would stay in the dormitories. There was a group of young people from around the world who had recently completed their doctorates and were there short-term to get some real-world experience (usually two years). The rest of the people were either research scientists, maintenance workers, or administrative staff that represented over thirty nationalities.

It was a pleasant place, but it was not the real Nigeria. Some people who lived on the site rarely ventured outside the fence. It was easy to imagine that the rest of Nigeria did not exist, and it was easy to stay inside the fence where it was safe. Compared to living in Lagos, it was comfortable. But it was also disturbing in its artificiality. The people who never left the site did not really experience living in Nigeria and lost out on a lot of interesting and wonderful experiences.

Outside the gates and down the road and past a military checkpoint, was the large sprawling village of Ibadan. At the time it had a population of 847,000 and was considered one of the largest villages in Africa. There were no skyscrapers, real financial district, or shopping malls. There was a large university, several outdoor markets, and a few shops. I loved to go shoe shopping because my feet were quite wide and the Nigerian women also had wide feet so I could finally find shoes that fit. And of course, the colorful Yoruba market women were there to bargain with.

In 1975, soon after my parents moved to Ibadan, there was a bloodless coup and General Yakubu Gowon was removed from office. He has lived in exile in the UK ever since. Since 1966, Nigeria has had eight coups or coup attempts. In 1976, there was a coup attempt when the head of state was assassinated and then the military took over and crushed the takeover. My father wrote:

> The military Head of State, General Murtala Ramat Muhammed (who had overthrown General Gowon) was assassinated in a bloody coup. When this happened, we were just finishing a workshop at IITA that was attended by many dignitaries from the United States and various African and European countries. This time, due to the violence of the coup, the military closed all borders, and no one was allowed in or out of the country for 10 days while they searched for the assassins. There also was a very strict curfew and travel within the country was curtailed. Fortunately, we were able to take care of our visitors and continue our research programs without interruption.
>
> However, we did have a problem with one of our senior staff members. This staff member, a Belgian, received word that his father had just died in Brussels, and he was determined to go home for the funeral. We tried, without success, to reason with him. He went to a vil-

lage on the border with Dahomey (now Benin) and hired a boat to take him secretly across the border. From there, he managed to get to Cotonou, the capitol, and caught a flight to Brussels. Of course, the military found out and the headlines next day said an IITA scientist had illegally crossed the border and was wanted for interrogation. To complicate the issue further, as soon as his wife knew that the military wanted to interrogate him, she came to our home and told me that her husband had two shotguns that he had brought into the country illegally and she didn't know what to do about them. She was certain that officials would soon be at her door to search her home. I did not think anyone would search our home, so after dark I went and moved the guns to our place. We knew that her husband would never be allowed back in Nigeria, so started arrangements for her and their children to pack up and depart the country as soon as possible. Later, we did move the guns back to her home. She packed them in the bottom of cases and their shipment left the country without trouble.

In total, my parents were in Ibadan for five years. I was lucky enough to spend time there and to see much of the Nigerian countryside.

SNAPSHOTS FROM NIGERIA

TRAVELING NORTH

We had two different drivers when we lived in Nigeria, both of them Muslims. They would usually have a pile of kola nuts on the dashboard. These were full of caffeine that helped them stay awake and stave off hunger. For some reason they even chewed on them during Ramadan (a time when Muslims fast). They were very bitter tasting and you only needed to bite off a little bit for it to have an effect. An extract from the kola nut was one of the original ingredients of Coca-Cola.

One summer a friend and I traveled by car from Ibadan to Kaduna and Kano in northern Nigeria. Kano was on the edge of the Sahara Desert and there was a big camel market just outside town with all kinds of scrawny looking camels. The Hausa tribe dominated in the north and they were Muslim. There were several mosques in Kano and we were interested in going into one of them but soon found out that women were not allowed. We were able to peek inside one and saw lush carpets on the floor and high arched ceilings. Most of the women on the streets were covered from head to foot in dark burkas. From time to time, we would see a woman who was not covered and we asked the driver about these women and who they might be. He said they were "useless women."

The market in Kaduna had large dye pits for dyeing cloth. We went deep into the market to see how the women tied the cloth for tie-dyed materials. The finished cloth was called *adire* and was a deep blue color. When we finally found the place, the women were not covered up. They were very interested in us and were happy to show us their tying techniques. They would take a small pebble and tie string around it in a circular pattern. It was amazing how fast they were. *Adire* is also made with stamped designs instead of being tied, and it is always a rich indigo color.

We then travelled to Benin City where there was a small museum near the university with the famous Benin bronze heads and other sculptures. This was what remained of a culture that had flourished between 1500 and 1800. The heads had delicate features and the artwork was much more sophisticated than what you saw in most places at the time. They used a process called the lost-wax process and mainly sculpted the heads of royalty.

Near the town of Osogbo we visited the Osun-Osogbo Sacred Grove. It was the center for women's fertility ceremonies and traditional healing on the Osun River. We were allowed into a private area and led down to the river to witness a ritual. There were many shrines in the area. An Austrian artist named Susan Wenger created sculptures, which were weird things that looked like huts or female forms. She partnered with local artists to revive the area and bring attention to it and today Osogbo is a UNESCO World Heritage site.

My mother was very interested in the Nigerian artists who were making a name for themselves at the time. She crossed paths with Twins Seven Seven, Bruce Onobrakpeya, Lamidi Olonade Fakeye, and David Dale and she promoted and purchased a lot of their work. My parents even donated two sculptures by Fakeye to the Minneapolis Institute of Art in 1995.

AFRICAN ANTS

One evening I was sitting on the porch in Ibadan, having a beer and bored out of my mind when I happened to glance at the floor. I panicked at the sight of ants at my feet; the ants in Africa are large and can be lethal. Fortunately, the ones I saw that night were not army ants. I think they must have been vegetarians.

I followed the river of ants and found they were coming out of the kitchen, across the dining room, over the sliding door tracks, onto the porch, and out a hole near the floor to the outside. I was mesmerized by them. Scouts ventured out at regular intervals to either check for danger or look for food. Then they would report back and another one would be dispatched. Pretty soon I noticed a potato chip moving across the floor. Several of them had hoisted it onto their backs and were carrying it out. I could not believe my eyes at first. After a while I saw another chip being hoisted in the same way.

This got me thinking. I just happened to be eating chips myself, although I'm pretty sure they were plantain chips. I wondered what would happen if I placed one where a scout might find it. Sure enough, a scout found it. He reported back and the river actually split off. None of them missed a step. They picked up the chip and rejoined the parade. I was amazed.

That same summer I went on a day trip to a large forest in western Nigeria with six other people in a pickup truck. The trip to the forest was pretty uneventful with the usual bickering between friends about the problems with transporting orchids. At one point, I was watching everybody gathered around a tree stump discussing the orchid growing on it when suddenly I realized I was being eaten alive by army ants.

Army ants have pincers instead of front legs. These carnivores can devour a lizard within seconds. The ants crawl up your legs inside your pants (unless you are smart and tuck your pants into your socks) and when they reach the thigh or pelvic area, they latch on. And they hurt! You can't just brush them off; you have to actually pull them off. I had to completely take my pants off to fully get rid of them all.

VILLAGE LIFE

Between my sophomore and junior year in college I spent the summer in Ibadan. I started hanging around a group of young American and British scientists. Francis was a Brit in his thirties with a wife and five children. He was thin, pale, and jittery and very focused on his work. David was a British entomologist who was in charge of gathering plants from all over Africa and putting samples of them into a living plant library. Ed was an American biochemist who spent his college days protesting the Vietnam War and then went into the Peace Corps. Then there was Simon, a British university student with long dark hair and a gorgeous smile. He had written asking for an internship and was told if he could get himself to Nigeria, he could have one. And so there he was.

We started going on Sunday outings just to get out into the countryside for a little adventure. On our first trip, we did some minor rock climbing, got stuck in the road a couple of times, and at one point, were accosted by a man wanting to know if Simon was a boy or a girl due to his long hair. Simon immediately jumped out of the car and started to take off his trousers. The man nearly went into hysterics, and we all had a good laugh.

At the end of the day, we stopped in a small village for some refreshment. There was no restaurant or store but, after having asked around, we found a house where the people were willing to sell us some beer. We sat on their porch and drank beer and the entire village came out to watch us. We found one young boy who spoke some English to be our translator. Pretty soon the family brought out dinner for us to share (fish curry and yam paste). Francis looked like he would be sick if he had to eat any of it. I tried some of the yam paste but left the curry to the others—I was sure it was extremely spicy. Everybody was getting quite drunk, and Simon was getting himself into trouble.

There was a young girl who lived in the house, and he was flirting with her a little bit. He told her father that he would love to have a farm in Africa. He asked the father if he had any land and the father said he did. He had some land over by the Dahomey border. Simon said he would be willing to consider marrying the daughter if he could have the land as a dowry. By the end of the evening, Simon was engaged to be married with a land deal in the making. I could not believe he had taken it as far as he did. Simon just said it did not mean anything and they would forget about it in the morning.

A week later, the girl showed up at the front gate of the compound with her brother to see Simon. Simon nervously tried to explain to them that it would not be possible for him to marry the girl. Her family was not happy; they said they would return with her father the next week. Simon and Ed prepared all week for what they would say to the man to get out of the deal. In the end, they were able to appease the family and convince them that Simon was a drunk and was not to be trusted. I'm sure some money changed hands.

CLIMBING ADO ROCK

We had heard of a village not too far from Ibadan where a huge rock was sitting in the middle of the plain; apparently after climbing it you could see for miles and miles. We decided it would be a good day's outing. Of course we did not have a map and only had sketchy directions, so we had to feel our way there, stopping to ask people who invariably had no idea what we were talking about and made up whatever they thought we wanted to hear.

At one such stop I was sitting in the back seat with Ed and smoking a cigarette. A group of women came up to my window and started pointing and laughing. I was feeling a bit paranoid and tense and could not figure out what was going on. Eventually we realized it must have been that women just did not smoke because we could see them mimicking me and laughing. After that we all had a good laugh.

We finally found Ado village and right next to it was Ado Rock. It must have been lodged there when the glacier receded, because landscape-wise, it was very out of place. The village was on just one side of the road and not very big. We walked through it and watched women weaving cloth and saw a group of children studying the Koran. As we got closer to the rock, we started to look for a path up. By this time, all the children of the village had latched on to us and started following us around. We asked them the way up, but they did not speak English and would just point in different directions. Finally, they led us to the chief's hut, and we realized we had to ask permission to climb the rock.

Apparently, the chief was building a new house and would welcome any contribution we could give him since he was generous enough to allow us to climb his rock. We told him we were just poor students and could only afford five naira (he wanted twenty), which was about eight dollars. He said that was not enough so we turned and started to leave, at which point, of course, he accepted the money. After some more discussion, he agreed to let us go alone without the children in tow. They showed us the path and left us to it.

The rock was flat on top but slanted up at one end. We climbed up at the lower end and worked our way to the higher side. Along the way, there were a couple of small ponds with vegetation around them. About two thirds of the way up, there was a small gully with trees and long grass. We could see vultures circling above this area and we were a little leery of crossing it. We also thought there might be snakes in the grass so Ed went first, making a lot of noise and clapping. I was last in line. Ed shouted back at me "It's usually the last person in line who gets bit, you know, Kathy." Very funny, Ed.

The view from up there was spectacular. You could see miles of green trees, bush, and flat land. It was so quiet and peaceful up there, I wanted to stay forever. We sat quietly and admired the view for a long time. On the way back, Simon took a dip in one of the ponds. Ed and I waited for him but Francis was in a huff because it was going to make us late getting back. I was supposed to be back by dark, but we almost always were late; Francis got blamed because he was driving and he was the only one who was responsible enough to care. Also he probably got some heat at home from his wife who was caring for those five kids alone all day.

Two years later Ed and I returned to Ado. I could not believe how much it had changed. The village had doubled in size and was now on both sides of the road. The chief had a big new house on the other side of town and the going rate for climbing the rock was forty naira—non-negotiable. We climbed up and had a picnic but did not go all the way to the other end.

When we came down from the rock, we had to go across a stream and through some bushes before coming out into the village. I was first in line and as I was going through the bushes I came upon a child alone on the path who must have been about two years old. When the child saw me, she started to scream—it was as if she had seen the scariest thing possible; she was terrified. Her mother came running up from the stream and picked up the child and started to laugh. Ed came up behind me and was laughing. I was confused. Finally, Ed caught his breath and said, "You are the first white person she has ever seen." And I realized he was right; she probably thought I was a ghost.

OUT ON THE TOWN

I'm not sure how it happened, but one evening a group of people were going out the door on their way to a local night club and they swooped me up along with them. The club was in a very large room with a dirt floor and a loud band at one end. It felt like I was in a large tent, but it might have actually had walls.

There were about seven of us. Francis was being very protective of me and kept making sure I was okay. This Nigerian guy went up to Francis and asked him if he could dance with me. Francis told him he would have to ask me himself. So, he came over to me and asked me to dance. I was getting ready to say no, thank you very much, when Simon started kicking me under the table and making gestures like I should really go dance. So being the nice person I am, I got up and danced with the guy. Big mistake there. By the end of the dance, he had asked me to marry him and ended up following us out to the car when we left and wanted to go with us.

We had all been drinking beer and about halfway through the evening I really had to go to the toilet. Everybody said I should just forget about it. I said, No really, I gotta go. So, David escorted me to the ladies' toilet. We went through a door and there were a lot of women just hanging around and two stalls with holes in the floor. There was no door or anything on the stalls. I went in and squatted, and David stood guard. It was not that terrible, partly I'm sure because I had had a few beers, but it was interesting. The women were obviously women of the evening just waiting for business. I did not get a chance to look around, but I assumed there were other rooms in the back for other activities. David seemed very nervous about the whole thing, and I was not allowed to drink any more beer after that.

BOSTON 1976

In the summer of 1976, I started to keep a journal and, in the fall, I took an English class in which keeping a journal was required. Since then, I have continued journaling off and on throughout the years.

> Feb. 6, 1977
>
> There is something wrong with my life and I don't know what it is. It might be that I have no roots. Most likely that's it. I'm sure that's it because it would complement my desire to settle down in one place and live and have

my own place and not move for a long time. But when I think of it, I wonder how long it would be before I got restless. But then again if I were happy, I shouldn't get restless at all.

I wrote this long before I knew about Third Culture Kids or that there were others who struggled like I did. In her book *Belonging Everywhere and Nowhere*, Lois Bushong wrote:

> For some TCKs you will see, however, a migratory instinct seems to control their lives—manifesting in frequent job changes, moves to new locations and constantly changing relationships. I believe that for them, a sense of rootlessness is at the heart of the restlessness. They can't settle down, even when they want to.

My junior year I decided I needed a break from Mills. My restless nature kicked in. Mills had an exchange program with several women's colleges on the east coast so I applied to Simmons College in Boston (now Simmons University). I was accepted and off I went. It was the American Bicentennial so it was a fitting place to spend it.

Simmons College was just down the street from Fenway Park where the Boston Red Sox played baseball, right in the middle of Boston. I could hop on the subway and be anywhere in minutes. I was just down the street from the Harvard Medical School so ambulances with sirens went screaming past my window day and night.

The first week of school, I saw flyers for a party. When I walked up to the door to buy a ticket, the Black girl sitting there told me it was for Blacks only. It was being sponsored by a Black organization and whites were not welcome. I said, "You're kidding, right?" She smiled and said "No." It seemed like she felt I was getting a taste of my own medicine. What a strange place this America was. So I went to the school's pub for a beer instead and ended up spending the evening with a Nigerian, an Italian who was half Ethiopian, a Sierra Leonean, a Frenchman who was half Algerian, and my friend Penny.

The next week there was a dance where whites were allowed (and Blacks too) and I met a cool guy named Chris. He was an engineering student who rode a British motorcycle and offered to show me around the Boston area since I had never been there before. I accepted and learned a lot about Americans through his eyes. For example, Boston was a very "ethnic" area where people had their own neighborhoods: Italian, Irish, Greek. He identified everybody by where their family had originally come from whereas I always just thought of people as American without really considering their country of origin.

In all my years of school, I had only had one year of US history and that was taken up mostly by the Watergate hearings. We visited many significant places like Concord, Salem, the Mayflower, Boston Commons, Bunker Hill, the Old North Church, Harvard Square, Cape Cod, and Walden Pond. It was probably the best American history education ever.

I had some interesting classes and I was amazed to find out that they took attendance and counted it as part of your grade, so for the first time in my college career I started to attend classes. I could not believe how easy school could be if you actually went to class. It saved all kinds of time making up for missed lectures. I found that I did not have to spend my time doing all that reading because they reviewed everything in the classroom and if I took notes I rarely had to study at all. I did a lot better in school that year and when I returned to Mills and attended classes my grades went up considerably. It was quite a revelation; I only wish I had discovered it sooner.

On the Fourth of July that year Arthur Fiedler led the Boston Pops concert on the Charles River Esplanade. We arrived early in the day and marked out our territory where we could see everything. By the time the concert started, the place was jammed and the police were getting irritable. Luckily, there were no major incidents, and it was a concert to remember. It ended with the *1812 Overture*, a cannon shooting over the Charles River, and an amazing fireworks show.

That summer I lived in Jamaica Plain, just outside Boston, in a two-bedroom apartment with Chris and my roommate from Simmons, Marla. I did temporary work in various offices around Boston. We took a couple of trips to Connecticut and New York City. One night we were out to dinner and Chris asked me to marry him. I said yes. But I told him I had to go back to California to finish my degree first. I was majoring in Spanish and their department was much better plus they had different requirements for graduation, so it made the most sense.

Chris and I met up at Thanksgiving and he told me he had had an affair with our summer roommate. He said it was nothing, a mistake. At the time I said it did not matter but I think it affected what came next. I went home to Nigeria for Christmas and met Frank. That was when I decided I could not marry Chris. It was not that I fell in crazy love with Frank—I did still love Chris—but I saw I was not ready to get married and settle down. I loved traveling and adventure and having the freedom to be with other people. I did not want to be a housewife and make babies. I broke it off with Chris. I broke his heart, and I was sorry for that but Mills taught me there were other options for women even though most of society still begged to differ.

My last year at Mills ended up not being all that great. I went a little wild and, since I had turned twenty-one, I spent a little too much time at the bars. I had a few one-night stands and of course, being drunk, precautions were not always followed. I found myself pregnant. Ugh. Twenty-one, still in school, no partner in sight, and pregnant. For me the solution was a no-brainer. I know it is a controversial subject, but I felt I had no choice. It was an impossible situation. This was four years after the *Roe v. Wade* decision that gave women the right to choose. I was able to end my pregnancy quickly, quietly, and legally. Hopefully, those days will return. My life would have been very different had I not been given that choice.

WINDING UP MY AFRICAN EXPERIENCE

It seems that my life has been filled with one bad plane experience after another. This time I was going home to Ibadan, Nigeria for Christmas in my senior year in college. I was supposed to go from San Francisco to Minneapolis to Chicago to Frankfurt to Lagos. The plane was late leaving Chicago, so I missed my connection in Frankfurt. When I went to the transfer desk, they told me that all the flights to Lagos that day were fully booked but they would keep trying. If they could not find a flight out that day there was one the next day out of Stockholm. I asked them to send a cable to my parents at the airport. Again, I had no money on me. I knew my mother would have gone down the night before and stayed at the guesthouse in Lagos near the airport, but I did not know the telephone number or the address there. I figured I would just have to play it by ear. If need be, I would try to get somebody from the airline to help me phone somebody although I did not know who.

I finally got a UTA flight out of Paris at midnight that was supposed to arrive in Lagos at 6:30 the next morning. UTA was a French airline that mainly flew to Africa (Union de Transports Aériens). I usually tried to avoid UTA because the pilots tended to get a little wild sometimes which made me even more nervous than usual, but I had no choice. As we approached the Lagos airport, it was pitch black and I thought there was probably a blackout or something. We came in for a landing and at the last moment the pilot pulled out and we circled around. He came on the loudspeaker and said that there was dense fog in Lagos and he was having trouble seeing but he would make another attempt. We made three attempts and all three times he pulled out at the last minute. Finally, he said that we were running low on fuel and since the plane was scheduled to go to Ghana anyway, we would go there and wait for the fog to lift.

In fact, there was no such thing as fog in Lagos. What the pilot saw was the Harmattan. Every year from November to March the winds blow south off of the Sahara Desert and the air becomes thick with sand. That is what he saw—sand—not fog.

After spending several hours in Ghana, we returned to Lagos and landed about 10 in the morning. The concept of queuing or standing in line in Nigeria was totally alien. When arriving at the Lagos airport, the procedure was to literally run for the first desk, which was passport control, and push to the front of the line. After reaching the desk, which was up on a platform, everyone waved his or her passport in the air trying to get the official's attention while standing in the stifling heat (no air-conditioning, of course). People everywhere jockeyed for position in the crushing crowd. From there, the next stop was a similar situation at the health control desk, to check for proper vaccinations. My brother came in once without having had his shots, and he spent a good two hours in the back room talking his way out of it. From there the next stop was the third circle of hell: luggage. There were always a million young boys wanting to help carry the bags and of course wanting a "dash" (or tip) for it. There was not any kind of fancy, mechanized conveyor belt. There was just a long line of steel rollers and after they were full, bags just fell off behind the counter.

I found my bags and deflected the luggage carriers, smiled at the customs officials who white chalked my luggage, and headed for the door. As I walked through, there was the usual lewd-sounding murmuring of "Taxi? Taxi?" to which I gave an appalled "No!" and moved through the crowd that hovered around the gate. As I came through, I looked around and there was my father's driver. He saw me right away and motioned to me. After that, he chased after my mother who was on her way out of the airport. Since I did not show up on the flight I was supposed to, she had met every plane from Europe but decided there was no way I would ever get on a UTA flight and thus had abandoned the idea of meeting that particular plane. Fortunately, I made it through customs before she left the airport and was able to catch her. It all turned out all right and we immediately hit the road up-country for Ibadan. It was eighty miles and I think the best time I ever made was four hours. If there was an accident it could take twice that long. The road was a rutted, narrow two-lane strip full of overloaded trucks and buses. Traffic was bumper-to-bumper. Passing was not an option unless you decided to take your life into your own hands.

This was my penultimate trip to Africa and I really enjoyed it. It was so vibrant. I was coming from California which was a very warm, alive place but Nigeria and its tropical climate was so intense, it impressed me more than before. I felt as if I could actually see the plants growing and flowering. I was glad to be in Africa and glad to be alive. Maybe it was the contrast of being in the US and then going back to Africa where I felt more comfortable. I just remember really enjoying my stay at "home" that vacation.

The University of Ibadan was right on the edge of town on the way out to my house. I met a veterinary student named Frank through my friend Ed. He was from Illinois, and he had not been able to get into vet school in the US, so he went to Nigeria. There were several Americans like him at the school, and he lived in a house on campus with a couple of other guys. He did not have a car, so he had to hitch and bum rides a lot before he got his motorcycle. One day he had hitched a ride with a truck driver, and he fell asleep because he was traveling some distance. He woke up with a jerk because the truck had come to a screeching halt and when he opened his eyes, he was staring down the barrel of a machine gun. The truck driver had run a roadblock.

One night Frank and I went to a party in town. He left his motorcycle at my house, and we took my mom's car. I was driving us home at about two in the morning. There were no streetlights, and the night was pitch black. I was feeling good, and I was really cruising down the highway when all of a sudden, I saw this lamp by the side of the road, and I immediately realized it was the roadblock. It was not where I expected it to be—plus, I had kind of forgotten about it. I slammed on the brakes and Frank was screaming at me, "Just keep going! Just keep going!" I skidded over to the side of the road and stopped. A Nigerian soldier came running up to the car and jammed his gun in through Frank's window. Frank was already starting the routine conversation: "So sorry, so sorry, we did not see you, very sorry, we did not see you, so very sorry."

The soldier was angry. He was screaming at us, and I was starting in on the "so sorry" routine but all I could think of was that I had no money on me so I could not bribe the guy and if he hauled me down to the police station, I could not remember my phone number and chances were that the phone would not work anyway. Nobody would know where I was, and God knew what they would do to me and what kind of a rat hole they would put me in.

After what seemed like an eternity, the soldier finally started to calm down. He was still gruff and angry but at least he had control of himself and took the gun out of Frank's face. We all knew these guys sat by the side of the road and smoked pot all night, so you never knew what kind of shape they were in. He started in with the usual questions: "Where are you going? Where have you come from? What do you have in the boot? Open the boot." So, I got out and opened the trunk and there was nothing there; he shone his flashlight around the car and finally he asked if Frank was sick. I thought it was an odd question. Then he said, "Drive on."

Frank was still shaking in the passenger seat when I pulled away and I guess I probably was too, but I was also thinking that the only thing that had saved us was the fact that I was driving because in asking me if Frank was sick, he was insinuating that there must be something wrong. Frank should have been driving. The guy had obviously surmised that I was just a dumb female driver who did not know any better.

Leaving Nigeria was no easier than the journey getting there. Once at the airport, the first thing was to check in with the airline and give over your luggage. Then it was to passport control, and to a room where they had gathered all the luggage. You had to identify your bags, answer questions, and sometimes the bags were opened and searched. This was obviously a bribe opportunity and it depended on the mood of the official whether you were to be singled out or not. Once the bags got the official chalked *x* on them, you then proceeded to the waiting room. There was no air-conditioning and only one gate. Once the flight was called, you walked through a metal detector, which nobody thought really worked. The plane was usually a short walk away outside and the luggage would be sitting on the tarmac. Military men with machine guns stood around. If anybody was stupid enough to pull out a camera, they would point their machine guns at you and start to shout. It was frightening. Everybody identified their own luggage before it was loaded onto the plane. After scaling the stairs to the plane, a flight attendant was waiting with gloves on to frisk each and every person. Nobody ever complained.

By the time my parents moved again after eight years in Nigeria, I was sad to go. Here was another chunk of my third culture. I loved the vibrancy of the African countryside, the outgoing friendly people, even the children who wanted to touch my strange hair. I loved the thick heat and the refreshing relief of the swimming pool. The spicy peanut stew, Star beer, plantain chips, chickpea bread, winged beans. The crazed confusion of the open market with its masses of people. The music, dancing, and singing. The toothy smiles. I would even somehow miss the unpredictable military men with machine guns. And the amazing sight of the sky at night with its so many stars, dots in the sky, like a vast painting of shapes and lights. It was an experience like no other.

PART FOUR

DENVER 1978

As my graduation from Mills approached, I started to panic. What was I going to do next? A BA in Spanish was not going to open a lot of doors. I decided I wanted to be a hotel manager in the South Pacific. Can you imagine a more idyllic job? And why not? So, I applied to Hotel and Restaurant Management School at the University of Denver and ended up working on a second bachelor's degree. Need I tell you how awful that was? Remember, this was 1978. I had just arrived from an all-women's college so I had a kind of skewed, idealistic view of the world. I walked into one of my first classes at Denver and the teacher looked around and said, "Five years ago there weren't *any* women in this class." I looked around. There were four of us. It kind of went downhill from there.

That first summer break, my cousin and a friend of mine from high school decided we would drive from Denver to Mexico City. People thought the idea of three white chicks driving 2,000 miles to Mexico City was crazy. It seemed like a perfectly normal thing to do to me. Jane, my cousin, flew in from Minneapolis and Tina, my high school friend flew in from San Francisco. We took my car—a VW Rabbit with a sunroof. We got lost in the Texas panhandle, but we made it to Austin and had a couple of days with Tina's family and friends. We went out dancing with some crazy gay guys I knew from boarding school. They were into taking ecstasy (MDMA) to enhance the dance floor experience. When we got to Laredo, we discovered a vial of it had ended up in my car so Tina threw it out the window in the middle of downtown.

We stopped at the border to go through customs and a Mexican border official came over to me and said something about how much stuff we had, and how he really did not want to bother us by making us take everything out. I said, "Hey, thanks." Then he leaned over real close and whispered, "*Mordida*."

"What?" I hesitated.

"*Mordida*," he repeated. I spoke fluent Spanish but for some reason his words were not registering because I could not wrap my head around the fact that I was really being asked for the *mordida* at the American border. I was surprised that he was being so forward.

"*Cuanto?*" (How much?) I asked.

He said, "*Pues, como puedes*" (Whatever you can).

I had no idea what the going rate was for bribing border guards, but I slipped a $20 bill into my passport and handed it to him. He took it gladly, and off we went.

Here we were, three American girls, on our way through the Chihuahuan Desert where the huge millipedes were like speed bumps that we hit every few feet. At one point my car started to overheat. We stopped and found that the radiator cap was missing. I had no idea how that could have happened. We pulled into a VW dealership on the outskirts of Monterrey.

We went round and round with the manager who said he could absolutely not give us a radiator cap because we were not his customers. If we had some work done on the car, then we could add the cap to the service, but he refused to sell us one. So, we went back out to the car. As we were getting ready to leave, a mechanic came running up to us and discretely handed me a radiator cap with a big smile on his face. He then walked away. It was very cool. We had arrived in Mexico for sure.

With our newly installed radiator cap, we pressed forward to Saltillo. We overnighted there and then began the trek across the desert to Mexico City. My cousin Jane did not know how to drive a stick shift, but we were not about to let her get away with not taking a turn at driving. We installed her in the driver's seat and every time she needed to shift, the person riding shotgun would deal with the gears. We jerked along, and the engine died every so often but mostly it worked.

At one point, we stopped for gas. We had noticed a sharp discrepancy between what it said on the pump and what the gas attendants were trying to charge us. This time we decided not to get ripped off again. We were going to pay what it said on the pump and to hell with them. Unfortunately, Jane was driving so this added a bit of challenge to the getaway plan. We paid the correct amount of money, Tina put the car in gear, and Jane floored it. We all held our breath hoping she would not kill the engine. We screeched out onto the highway and luckily did not run into any trucks in the process. Success! We did, however, keep a watch behind us for a while to be sure they were not coming after us with *pistolas*.

Our plan was to stay with Alicia, an old friend of my family in Mexico City. I had no idea where she lived or how to get there so I just drove into the city and kept going until I got to an area I recognized. I could not believe the traffic; there was total gridlock in some areas. I finally found a pay phone and pulled over. Alicia gave me directions and I had to get onto the *periférico*, which was the highway that went through Mexico City. It was a crazy road, several lanes wide, where people usually went way too fast. As I was trying to merge onto it, I soon realized that nobody was going to let me in and the only thing to do was just shut my eyes and go.

Alicia lived in a high-rise condominium near the university. I parked the car on the street outside and we went in. The next morning, I came out and every single piece of chrome on my car, including the hubcaps, was gone. At least they had left the car—and the radiator cap.

We had a very pleasant time sightseeing and wandering around Mexico City. The only negative experience was on the subway. We jumped onto a car jammed full of men. Jane and Tina managed to make their way over to the window and somehow found seats. I stayed nearer to the door because the whole car was so full.

Soon the men closed in around me and there were a million hands all over me. I looked around to see who the guilty parties were and everyone I looked at was staring at the ceiling. Finally, I decided I had to take some action. I managed to get my elbows perpendicular to my body and I rotated with as much force as I could. They all scattered to the far corners of the car, which made us all laugh. I then managed to make it over to where my friends were. When we got back to the condo, we found out there were separate subway cars for men and women to reduce groping. We felt pretty stupid to have not known that.

The city I had grown up in had changed, but I still loved every minute of it. It felt familiar, like home.

MINNEAPOLIS 1980

Back in Denver, I got about halfway through my second year of school and decided it was a battle I did not want to fight; I did not enjoy it. I was taking a class in finance and had no idea what it was about. I could not follow it. I also had a class in sales; I was sick once and missed a few lectures but nobody would give me their notes. One requirement for that class was to go on a sales call with somebody in the business. I managed to set one up, but I was a few minutes late because I could not find a parking space and she left without me. An executive from one of the major international hotel chains came to speak to one of my classes. Towards the end, somebody asked him how many women managers they had. His answer was: "We are definitely open to the idea." Oh my god, I thought. Seriously? What a pompous ass. I decided enough was enough and I was never going to be a hotel manager. I was depressed and demoralized and just wanted it all to end.

I still had no plan for gainful employment but since everything I owned would fit into my VW Rabbit, I dropped out of school, packed up my car, and drove to Minnesota to live with my brother. Upon arriving in Minneapolis, of course my first goal was to get out of town. So, I decided that in the short term, I would work at any old job and save up enough money to go spend some time in Scotland, which was something I had always wanted to do. I went to work in a restaurant and made salads for six months.

In the meantime, my parents were moving to the Netherlands. My father was to be the founding Director of the International Service for National Agricultural Research in The Hague. They invited me to go and stay with them and help them get settled. That worked out great because I figured I could travel around Scotland until my money ran out and then head over to the Netherlands.

My cousin, Jane, was studying in London that summer and I managed to talk her brother into going to Scotland with me. I flew in and spent a couple of days with Jane before her brother, Steve, arrived. We did not really have a plan but just jumped on the next train to Edinburgh. On the train there were two seats facing forward and two seats facing backwards with a table in the middle. Toward the end of the trip a Scotsman sat down across from me. When he found out that we really did not know where we were going, he started hauling out maps and planned an entire trip for us in the western islands. He told us about good places to go and it was awesome. He was a really nice guy. Really half the fun of travel is the people you meet.

After seeing some of the sights in Edinburgh we took the train to Inverness. We could not get into the youth hostel, so we ended up in a bed-and-breakfast. There were bibles all over the house. The woman who owned it kept giving us furtive glances probably because we were sharing a room but had different last names. We thought we should tell her we were cousins but then we decided that might not really help too much. She was glad to see the back of us.

The following day we took the bus to Drumnadrochit and walked from there to Urquhart Castle right on Loch Ness. There was not much left of the castle because it was blown up to keep the Jacobites from staying there (to make a long story short). I did not see the Loch Ness Monster. Such a big disappointment for me!

Back in Inverness, we went to the pub at the Old Market Inn and had a few beers. One drunk Scotsman sort of latched on to us. He mainly just wanted to talk to someone—anyone would have done—but we were willing to listen to him. What he talked about was interesting enough, some Scottish history and very strong opinions. After a while somebody got up with a guitar and started singing folk music, which we quite enjoyed.

From Inverness, we took the bus through the mountains past glass-still lakes, hilly open areas, fields of sheep, and lush green forests on to Fort William. What struck me most about that bus ride was the open emptiness. We saw a lot of sheep but no people. Years later I had a similar experience riding a bus through Patagonia. Miles and miles of sheep and empty spaces. No billboards, no signs, just space. There was such peace.

The youth hostel was outside Fort William at the foot of the highest mountain in the UK, Ben Nevis (4,413 ft). A New Zealander latched onto us at the youth hostel, which was a good thing because he had dishes and silverware and we had come totally unprepared. I think he was homesick. We ended up taking him into town and waving goodbye at the bus station like he was our son going off to war, poor guy. We spent a couple of days there hiking, relaxing, and soaking up the beautiful countryside before heading out to the west coast.

We were lucky that it rained very little that summer. The only problem we had was on the Isle of Skye. The public transport was rather meager, so we were trying to hitchhike when, of course, it started to rain and we got soaked. Back on the mainland, we worked our way down the west coast to Oban where we took day trips out to several islands including Mull and Iona. I fell in love with Scotland and decided I wanted to go back someday and tour the upper peninsula on a motorcycle (or really on the back of a motorcycle).

We stopped briefly in Glasgow but I did not like the vibe there, so we hopped on a train going south and ended up in the old Roman town of Chester on the Welsh border. From there it was on to Stonehenge and Salisbury. It was market day in Salisbury and there were people everywhere, crowding the streets. I was tired by then and it was too much for me. Youth hostels were cheap, but I did not get much sleep. The woman above me had snored all night. Still, I was able to enjoy Salisbury Cathedral, an impressive Gothic structure that was finished in 1258. We listened to the music at the evensong service.

We slept on somebody's floor in London and stayed with a friend in Milton Keynes after cruising through Oxford. We ended the tour with a boat ride across the channel from Great Yarmouth to the Hook of Holland and then a train on to The Hague. We got off at the wrong station and had to walk forever but finally managed to hook up with my parents and ended up staying in their new empty apartment.

I stayed in The Hague for three months working for my dad and helping my mom find her way around the city. It was a nice break. That December, I flew back to Minneapolis, ready to find a job and strike out on my own.

I ended up spending nine years in Minneapolis; for the most part I liked it. It was easy to live there with family nearby and plenty to do. I joined the art museum and took a class. I always wanted to take classes in some subject or another, but I would usually start out with enthusiasm and good intentions and then kind of fizzle out and not finish them. I blamed it on the long winters or some other reason.

During that time, I took a trip to southern Spain that met all of my expectations. Having majored in Spanish and studied Spanish history and literature for many years, it was rewarding to finally see everything in person. I had been to Madrid and to the Prado Museum during my Switzerland days, but my main interests were in Andalusia. I spent two glorious weeks in Seville, Córdoba, and Granada. When I was growing up in Mexico, I had been in love with a bullfighter from Córdoba. He was called El Cordobés, and in his hometown, there was a museum dedicated to him.

I spent two full days at the Alhambra Palace in Granada. In the Generalife Palace, intricately laid out patterns of trellised roses were in full bloom. The overwhelming smell of jasmine came out of nowhere. Hints of lavender, thyme, and rosemary lingered in the air. The palace mosaics were so detailed and beautiful. Afterward I felt like I had completed a pilgrimage. And yet after I had seen it, I did not feel a need to return. It's funny how some places haunt you, pulling you back and others release you.

I returned to Minneapolis and spent the summer working a part-time job on the weekends at the Home Shopping Network in addition to my full-time job. I took the job not really knowing too much about the industry. I thought it was some kind of new fad that would die out. The surprising thing was how many people were up at 7 AM on Sunday morning and ready to shop. In some ways, it was pure Americana and pure materialism, except that since I was a bilingual telemarketer, most of my clients were Hispanic.

I entered a world that I could never have imagined. I was part salesperson, part therapist. Many people would call to buy something but really, they just wanted somebody to talk to. They would tell me everything about themselves and their children and their grandchildren. I could not really talk to them for long because I had to make that next sale. I do not think it improved my Spanish much, but I learned a little more about people and some of the crazy things they do. One woman lived in a trailer in New Mexico with 104 porcelain dolls. She was so excited to buy the 105th one from me. It was sad, really.

In September 1985, after thirty years of living abroad, my parents moved to Minneapolis to begin their retirement. That was when the one trunk with my treasures disappeared for good. I had assumed it would continue to follow me around, but my parents felt I had not shown enough interest in it and threw it out. My Japanese doll was in it among other things. There went the remains of my childhood.

My father continued to do consulting work for ten years after he retired. This took him to Nigeria, Chile, the Dominican Republic, Brazil, Uganda, Indonesia, Zimbabwe, China, Thailand, Costa Rica, the Philippines, Malawi, Tanzania, Pakistan, Nepal, and India. He saw ninety countries by his ninetieth birthday. Not bad for a guy who grew up during the Great Depression on a farm in southern Iowa, as the youngest of seven children.

MARRIAGE

I dated several men in Minneapolis but was not serious about any of them. In the Midwest, it was difficult for me to find people I could relate to; there weren't many global nomads around. Many of the people I met were very provincial and had never been out of the state let alone out of the country, nor did they want to. One day, however, a personal ad in the back of the weekly newspaper caught my eye: "Speak one foreign language, learning another, travelled to Central America, eclectic taste in music, a writer." We met in a German restaurant over a bottle of Liebfraumilch and then he and I took a walk around one of the many lakes in Minneapolis to get to know each other.

Nicholas was born in Milwaukee, Wisconsin. His parents were immigrants from the USSR after World War II. He grew up speaking Russian at home and became his father's translator at an early age, since his father had never learned to speak English very well. Nicholas had a yen to return to his homeland. The only relatives he had in the US were his immediate nuclear family, but he knew that he had relatives still living in the USSR—his uncle and several cousins in Moscow, an aunt and a cousin in St. Petersburg, and another aunt and cousin in Ukraine.

It was not love at first sight. He had just returned from Nicaragua where he had suffered a bout of dysentery, and he was as skinny as a rail. His hair was jet black, very straight and short. But his eyes were like Omar Sharif's in *Dr. Zhivago*, dark brown pools you just wanted to dive into.

After dating off and on for four years, I fell crazy in love with him. He was creative, seductive, unpredictable, and adventurous. I could not resist him. We were married in December 1988. After our honeymoon in the Yucatán, Nicholas left to spend a month in Russia, his first of many trips. Not long after he got back, he landed a job as a reporter at a paper in Florida. He headed out first to find us a place to live in Dunedin, Florida, which was to be our new home.

FLORIDA

My brother's wife, Jennifer, and I set out from Minneapolis to join Nicholas with all our belongings in an eighteen-foot rented truck. On a late afternoon in August my family and friends came out to help pack it up. The next day at 6 AM, we started out.

We went out of our way to avoid Chicago, but we did have to cut through a small corner of it. It was about 100° so we had the windows wide open (since there was no air-conditioning) and Jennifer was playing the radio full blast, trying to find a mellow station to calm us both down. There were semi-trucks passing us on both sides going about 80 miles an hour while I was trying to keep the truck at 55 (although I really wanted to just go 30).

It was a big truck; the first time we stopped for gas, Jennifer almost took out one of the pumps and then nearly backed over a dumpster. Being aware of your surroundings is very important while driving large trucks. We made it a team effort with one of us directing and the other driving, which worked.

When we crossed into Tennessee, we hit a weigh station right away. We pulled over and stopped at the scale. The man in the booth yelled over the microphone that we should pull around to the rear. When we asked what was up, he said, "It's the boys in blue around the corner," with just a slight smirk on his face. The boys in blue must have been very bored. They wanted to have a look see at the "girly" driving the truck. They asked, "What do you have in there? Just your personal belongings?" with a lot of smiling all around. We played along because we wanted to get out of there, but this confirmed my "good old boy" view of the South. It certainly did not make me want to hang around.

Just before reaching Chattanooga, Tennessee, there was an especially steep mountain that we had to go down. At the top, all trucks had to pull over and look at the maps of the road to see where the emergency ramps were. These ramps ended in a lot of sand and were there in case you lost control and had no other way of stopping. We were also told how fast we should be going according to the size of the truck. We white-knuckled it most of the way down but kept everything under control. Nicholas later told me that when he drove down, he saw somebody buried in an escape ramp sand pile.

On our way into Atlanta, we watched the lunar eclipse, and we were parking the truck at the motel just when it reached blackout. It was really something to see; I had never watched one for that long before. It kept us company, diverted us, and at the same time, had a calming effect.

On the third day, we reached Florida. The billboards immediately changed. "Call now for your Disney World tickets," "Cheap lodging at Disney World," "Discounts for Disney World," "Orlando, Dawn of the New Age," "Mickey Lives," "Rides, Rides, Rides," and "Ride till you Puke!" Well, we were just about to puke, so we decided to take our chances and get off the main road. We cut cross-country from Gainesville on to a narrow two-way highway through farm country and small rural towns. We came out on the other side to a kind of run-down four-lane highway that took us right into Dunedin.

We unpacked the truck in the wet summer heat of Florida, a heat that slapped you in the face like a steam bath the minute you walked out the door. It reminded me of being in Lagos again. The sweat dripped down my scalp and into my eyes, so I had to wear a headband to even be able to see.

We spent a year and a half in Dunedin, which I affectionately called a cultural wasteland. Just before they could fire Nicholas from his glamorous job as a suburban reporter in Florida, our lives changed forever: he got an offer of a job in Moscow, Russia.

WASHINGTON, DC

In November 1989, we watched the Berlin Wall come down and saw Gorbachev promote Glasnost and a more open and friendly Soviet Union. Nicholas began to see his dream of working and living in Moscow might be possible now. He answered a random ad and was offered a job in Moscow, writing for a start-up publication. They sent us a cash advance so we could pack up our things and ship some of them over. All we needed were our visas and we were on our way. It was just before Christmas, so we loaded up the car and drove to Minnesota to say goodbye to our families.

After Christmas things were stalled, so we drove to Washington, D.C. to find out what the problem was. It soon became clear the job just was not going to happen. The start-up had lost their funding and could not fulfill their offer to Nicholas. And so there we were in D.C. with no jobs, all our stuff in storage in Florida, and several boxes in a warehouse waiting to be shipped to Moscow. It was a fine state of affairs. But ultimately, we were happy to be out of Florida and it was exciting to be in D.C. with all the culture and civilization it had to offer.

I started working temp jobs and Nicholas started freelancing. After a horrible month in a rented room, we scraped up enough money together to rent an apartment and get our boxes out of the warehouse. About six months later, I landed a government job and Nicholas left for Moscow to work as a freelance journalist in print and radio.

It was August 19, 1991, a Monday morning, my day off. I had been up until 1:30 AM the night before and my alarm went off at 5:30.

I usually just turned it off, but on this morning I got up and switched it over to the regular NPR channel, which was on from 5:30 to 6:00 AM. Right away I heard, "…tanks rolling on the streets of Moscow…" and then a break for a public service announcement.

I jumped out of bed and ran to the computer to check my email. There was a short message from Nicholas that there had been a coup d'état and that I should call a couple of people to let them know that he was on the scene, available for reporting. Relieved, I went back to bed to listen to the radio.

At 6 AM, Morning Edition came on and Bob Edwards announced the Soviet overthrow. The next voice I heard was Nicholas, reporting live from Moscow. Wow! He sounded like he was on speed, he was talking so fast. He was really pumped up. As I listened, slowly the story unfolded. Gorbachev had been detained in Crimea and there was a "Gang of Eight" taking over the government and the army had moved in to keep everybody under control. Nicholas called and said he was fine and there had been no shooting. I heard him again later in the newscast and he sounded much calmer.

That week I went to a German friend's house and her mother talked my ear off telling me all about her trip mostly on foot across China while pregnant during World War II. They had lived in China for twenty years and were there during the Japanese occupation. After telling me all of these horror stories, she had the gall to tell me not to go to Russia because it was "dangerous." I was amazed at her perspective.

The attempted coup in Moscow was over quickly. The junta was in custody. People were dancing in the streets of Moscow. It all really brought tears to my eyes. This was a real chance for democracy there and Nicholas had witnessed it firsthand. His timing was right. He was hired on at Marketplace on a trial basis. I hoped things would continue to go well for him and I wished I could be with him. I missed him a lot and I would have liked to be able to share it all with him. Nicholas had been toasting Boris Yeltsin every evening with his cousin, so I toasted Boris, too. It was history in the making.

MOSCOW

In October 1991, I arrived in Moscow for my first visit. Nicholas was living with his cousin and when we got to their apartment all his relatives were waiting for us. There was Valery, Valya, and Raisa, three of Nicholas's cousins with their spouses and children. Also, Nicholas's uncle, Alexander, and his wife, Lena. We had a feast of cucumber and tomato salad, wild mushrooms with onions, salami, cheese, bread, pickled squash, sprats, two bottles of Champagne, and a bottle of cognac. We sat and talked for a while and then came potatoes and meat with carrots. It was all very good. Then more cognac, tea, and dessert—chocolates and éclairs stuffed with whipped cream. Right after dinner the guests left.

After meat and potatoes with coffee for breakfast the next morning, Nicholas and I walked down to Red Square and saw Lenin's tomb. Once inside, nobody was allowed to have their hands in their pockets, and the guards made sure the line moved quickly, no dallying allowed. Lenin was in a glass case and all you saw was a head and two small hands poking out of a large suit. He looked waxy in the dim light. It was weird.

Moscow was a drab city. There was color but it was faded. It reminded me of the older parts of Mexico City when I had first moved there thirty years ago. The city was dusty, dirty, and worn-down; the tarmac sidewalks were falling apart. The air was filled with bad car fumes and everybody's cigarette smoke. Muscovites drove fast and erratically, and pedestrians did not have the right-of-way. Luckily, there were underground passages for crossing multi-lane roads.

Back at Valery's apartment, everyone sat around a small table in the kitchen drinking tea. It turns out that Russians drank more tea than the British. They paid a flat fee for gas and water, so they did not care how much of it they used. Often the stove's gas burners were just left on so they would not have to be relit or simply to keep the kitchen warm.

On a typical night, Valya would be out hitting up different stores, looking for whatever she could find. One night she called to say she had found some cognac but needed to return an empty bottle in order to get any. We collected the empties and headed to the store to meet her. We even got lucky and found some herring and a sturgeon's head (even though it was frozen solid), which they said would make good soup.

We took a day trip to Zagorsk, about forty miles to the northeast of Moscow. Zagorsk, originally known as Sergiyev Posad, was home to the Holy Trinity Lavra of St. Sergius, the most important Russian monastery and the spiritual center of the Russian Orthodox Church. The monastery was originally built in the 1200s. It started as a church and a walled city and evolved into a seminary and monastery church complex. There was also a holy spring within the walls where people from all over came on pilgrimages to get the water. It was the seat of the Russian Orthodox Church all through the communist years.

During our visit, there was a mass going on in the main cathedral and the priest was singing with a full choir doing the response. The nave was lit only with candles and the air was thick with incense. It was crowded, stuffy, and suffocating. At the back there were three windows with priests selling candles. Frescoes adorned the walls and ceiling and icons were painted on the iconostasis. When they opened the Tsar's doors you could see to the other side, and it looked like the cathedral went on forever with lines of gold pillars tapering into the distance. It was breathtaking.

Back in Moscow, I saw the changing of the guard at Lenin's tomb and then wandered around GUM (the big state department store) on Red Square. In the afternoon, we went to the Tretyakov Museum. At the back, we found the remains of the statues the masses had toppled after the coup. There were lots of Lenin's and Stalin's, all at random angles.

Later that night, a little after 12:30, I heard the doorbell ring. Well, nobody answered it, so it rang again. Finally, I got up and unlocked the door and there was Valery—totally wasted and looking like he had crawled through the mud. He had been out at a party where they were drinking pure grain alcohol, and he had fallen on the way home. He went to bed fully clothed and was still in bed when we left at about 1 PM the next day.

On the morning I left Moscow, the alarm went off at 5:30 AM and I woke up to my churning bowels aka Stalin's Revenge or whatever they called it in Russia. Ugh. I was flying Aeroflot to Helsinki. The plane was a rickety old thing. As I walked up the aisle, I was glad I wasn't wearing spike heels because it felt like they would probably have gone through the floor. The seats were all worn and old-fashioned. I was sitting by an emergency exit and there was no legroom at all. If there was an emergency, people would have had a hard time getting through to the exit window. There was a choice of about four different beverages; the only thing I understood was lemonade and so I asked for that, but it turned out to be more of an apple-like, frothy beverage that looked like beer—probably kvas. When I declined a breakfast tray, I was given this look like I was out of my mind. I guess not too many people turned down food. I was just glad when we finally landed in Helsinki.

My trip to Russia was short and I mostly just saw touristy things, but it did give me a taste of the place and introduced me to Nicholas's relatives. Overall, I did not love it.

PART FIVE

ARRIVAL 1993

I spent two years in Washington, D.C. with my husband running around Moscow by himself. The problem was he was having way too much fun without me and was dragging his feet when it came to our relationship. After much back and forth and Sturm und Drang I decided to join Nicholas in Moscow in April 1993. I thought maybe it would work out between us and maybe it would not. But for some dumb reason I still cared for him and figured I would give it a try. Plus being a TCK, I had itchy feet to go somewhere else and figured, why not Russia? I did not have any particular burning desire to go live there long-term but it was a time when history was in the making and I thought it might be fun to be a part of it.

My parents were having their fiftieth wedding anniversary that year and I had promised my brothers I would be there for the occasion. I arrived in Minneapolis a week before I was due to leave for Russia, having once again packed everything up, put it into storage, and sold a lot of furniture and appliances. I was so sick of moving, I just tried to get rid of as much stuff as I possibly could. My biggest challenge was selling the car. That process came down to the wire and I was afraid I was going to have to give the thing away, but I managed to unload it a few days before I left Washington. On Saturday we had a nice anniversary dinner for my parents and on Sunday my father gave me a box of Valium and sent me on my way. (He always stocked up when he traveled to India where it was readily available. It was mainly for my mother to help on long flights. I never liked it much but took the box just in case.)

I landed in Moscow totally green. It was one of the few times in my life I did not do my homework on a place first. I had been pulled back and forth for almost two years. Should I go or should I stay? When I finally made the decision to move, I had not convinced myself it would be permanent. I thought of it as an adventure that might only last a short time. I was determined to not make any long-term plans.

My husband had a job with an American company with some benefits but not much. He was the only expat in the office that he ran. I figured it was a good time for me to move since I would have some kind of net under me. As a child, my father always had a good job with an international organization that provided comprehensive benefits and helped us get organized and adjusted to new places. There was always a built-in support system. This was something I did not have when I moved to Moscow. The only people I knew were my husband and his Russian family, who spoke no English. I had this vision that his family would take me under their wing, show me around, help me navigate the markets, and take me sightseeing. This did not happen.

Landing in Moscow, I was totally out of my element. I had no idea what was in store for me. On arrival, I slogged through customs to the other side where I was greeted by Nicholas, attached to a car and driver. The driver was a new Russian entrepreneur who was in the business of renting out holiday apartments to tourists and providing transportation. A couple from Delaware were already there with several large bags. The car was small so it was a tight squeeze. They call them Ladas, but they are really small Fiats made in Russia. Some luggage ended up strapped to the roof. The couple from Delaware were in shock. They obviously didn't expect to share a car. Neither did I, for that matter; I had visited once before but this time it would be permanent, sink or swim. I thought to myself, Hold on to your hat.

After a harrowing ride with all the windows wide open and being crushed in the back seat, we emerged in front of our apartment building. The Soviets built big ugly concrete apartment buildings in blocks. Each block had several entrances. The entrance to our section of the building stank of old garbage and the floor was dirty. The only light bulb was either gone or burnt out so it was dark. The walls were covered in graffiti. The lift could fit only four people at the most and we barely fit in with my luggage. The buttons for the floors were melted like somebody had taken a lighter to them, but amazingly enough they still worked.

Nicholas had rented our two-room apartment from an elderly lady who had left everything she owned right where it was. The place was packed with all her furniture, dishes, knickknacks, books, and kitchen stuff. There was an open fold-out couch in one room which would be our bed. There were no real closets, so it looked like I would be living out of my suitcases. The kitchen had a small refrigerator, an oven with stovetop, a sink, and a table with benches, small but functional. There were separate rooms for the toilet and bathroom (with a bathtub plus a sink). The windows that opened were small and had no screens. The living room had a dining table, an old uncomfortable satin couch, a couple of chairs, and floor-to-ceiling glass shelves (most of them locked). Nicholas was using a trunk he had shipped as a coffee table. Plus, he had purchased a TV, so it sat prominently across from the couch. The room was so full of junk, you could barely move.

LEARNING TO BUY BREAD

My first year in Moscow there were five main grocery stores that I would go to. They were all fairly small compared to American stores, but they were probably average compared to European ones. One was Finnish, one German, two Irish, and one near our house that did not seem to have any specific affiliation. I had to hit up all of them at least once a week in order to keep on top of what was available at the moment. Some stores carried certain items that others did not, but it was totally unpredictable. It all depended on when their shipment arrived.

If I had spoken Russian, I could have gone to the farmer's market and found vegetables cheaper, but Nicholas did not seem interested in that. I do not know if he just did not want to deal with it or if he really did not trust Russian food. He said he did not want to buy Russian eggs because you could never be sure whether they came from Ukraine and could be radioactive. It was seven years after Chernobyl, but that was not so long in nuclear years. When I first got to Moscow, Nicholas gave me a Geiger counter he had found in one of the street markets but I never used it.

The grocery stores I went to were called "hard currency" stores. Everything was priced in dollars and you had to pay in dollars or by credit card. There was usually somebody who spoke English but not always. In the Russian stores, they never spoke English. The buying process there was rather complicated: you had to decide what you wanted, go tell the cashier (who sat in a cubicle) the cost of the item and the lot number, and return with the receipt to claim the goods. I could never figure out what the lot number was.

There was a bakery right outside our apartment building. I knew it was a bakery because it always smelled so good. Fresh bread in the middle of winter sounded great. I went in one day to check it out and it was packed with people. I stood and watched as people went up to the counter, looked around, and then queued up at the cashier's cage. They would tell the cashier the name of the bread they wanted, how many, and what it cost—at least that is what I assumed was going on, as the exchange was all in Russian.

Over the next few days, I stopped in on my way home and watched this process, trying to catch the names of the bread people were buying. I still could not make out the Cyrillic writing under the loaves. I finally managed to catch the name of one of the loaves—*bulochki*; it was like a small, fat French or Italian type of bread. I decided to give it a try. I got in line for the cashier and yelled, "*Odin bulochka!*" into her cage. I had learned how to count to ten and felt confident that *odin* meant "one." Much later I learned that Russian is more complicated than Latin and there were different ways of saying "one" depending on what you were talking about. I should have said *odna*.

Of course, she did not understand me and started to yell at me. I quickly left the building. A few days later, I waited until there were only a few people in the store. Using a combination of sign language and my rudimentary language skills, I asked the woman behind the counter what the bread was called that I was pointing to. She told me. I asked her how much it cost. She realized I was not catching on too quickly, so she kindly wrote it all down for me on a piece of paper. I went to the cashier and handed her the paper. I paid the amount and returned to the counter with my receipt to collect my bread. I had successfully purchased my first loaf of bread in Russia. I was so happy. I felt like I should frame it or something. Success tasted delicious.

I went through this process many more times during my years in Russia but eventually my language skills improved and my rudimentary skills were honed enough that I could make transactions without falling apart. Often this involved interactions with the Russian Babushka figure, a fearsome entity. She was a grandmother who wore a scarf on her head and was always telling you, "You should button your coat," "You should not sit on marble," "You should wear a hat," "Your son should put his gloves on," or "What is wrong with you! Why don't you do what I say?" She was everywhere and she was intimidating. These were the women who controlled the cashier stations in the Russian shops.

As time went by, the hard currency stores changed and grew. The Finnish grocery store expanded into a full three-story department store with a big grocery section in the basement. Many of the smaller stores closed but others opened. Supermarkets were born and for the most part I could find anything I wanted—for a price.

At one point we lived near the city's largest outdoor market. I would go down there just to look around and sometimes I would buy fruit or vegetables. It was huge and had all kinds of spices, nuts, fruits, cheeses, types of honey, and vegetables. Many of the vendors were men who came from the south—Kazakhstan, Azerbaijan, or Georgia. They wanted to bargain over everything. Over time I came to appreciate these *rynoks* and shopped there more often as I became more comfortable with my Russian.

I usually avoided the meat and fish since there was no refrigeration and it was all hacked apart in front of you with giant cleavers, with strong fishy smells, flies hovering, and blood dripping. It made me queasy to walk through that section. I just was not adventurous enough for that plus I did not know my cuts well enough. They also had large vats of caviar for sale, which I also avoided since (a) I did not know a lot about caviar and (b) again, there was no refrigeration.

You knew you were entering the pickled food section when the overwhelming smell of garlic attacked your senses. Everything was available pickled. You could find pickled green and red tomatoes, whole garlic bulbs, cucumbers, peppers, cabbage, grape leaves, and the long green stalks of the garlic plant. Other vendors offered Korean salads made from carrots, eggplants, meats, fish, and other ingredients.

Russians were also huge mushroom and berry eaters. I could always find all kinds of berries in summer to make delicious pies and breads. There was always a big section of honey, honeycombs, walnuts packed in honey, and beeswax candles for sale. You could often get a taste for free. All kinds of nuts were for sale and since pine nuts grew in Siberia, they were relatively inexpensive and readily available.

EATING OUT

When I arrived in 1993, Moscow was home to the world's largest McDonald's. It was a big two-story building on Pushkin Square. There was always a line going down the block no matter what time of day it was. After my son was born in 1995, we often went to McDonald's to get the Happy Meal. He could pick out the free gift he wanted and dip his French fries into his milkshake.

There was also Patio Pizza, opened by a Venezuelan named Rostislav Ordovsky-Tanaevsky Blanco, who we all called Rostik. It was an instant hit. Until then, there were a few Irish pubs and some very expensive hotel restaurants but not much more. By the time we left, he had opened about twenty restaurants including a couple of TGI Fridays. He made his fortune.

My husband belonged to a group of expats in Moscow who had all grown up outside of Russia but all had Soviet parents. They grew up speaking Russian, going to Russian Orthodox Church, and Russian camp in the summer. They were from the US, Venezuela, Argentina, and other places. Rostik was one of them and we would all meet at one of his restaurants a couple of times a year for blini, drinks, and lots of toasts. It was fun. You never knew who would be there and they were all interesting people.

As time went on, there were more places to eat out around town. A couple of guys bought an old diner in the US and shipped it to Moscow. They served hamburgers and milkshakes, of course. There was a

Swiss restaurant right on the river that served fondue and one night we went to a Finnish restaurant and had reindeer carpaccio. We also discovered some nice small Russian restaurants that served excellent borscht and flavored vodka and ate at many very expensive upscale Russian restaurants, too.

By the time I left in 2001, there were something like thirteen McDonald's around the city. The lines were not as long as when they had first opened, but they were all packed most of the time.

GETTING AROUND MOSCOW

While living in Moscow, I had to rely on public transportation, but it took me a while to get up the guts to get out on my own and tackle the metro and the buses. Every time I went out, I became braver and learned something new. In the metro, all the signs were in Russian only so I would have to sit down and concentrate to figure out what the Cyrillic writing said to know which way to go.

People were always coming up to me on the street or in the metro or on a bus and asking me things. I had no idea what they were saying and I usually said, "I do not understand," "I do not know," or "I do not speak Russian." Eventually I figured out that on the metro most of them were asking me if I was getting off at the next stop because they wanted to position themselves for the exit.

During the whole nine years I lived in Moscow, we only had a car for about nine months. Nicholas bought a Russian Jeep—a red Niva—and drove it around for a while. He soon discovered that the special plates they put on all cars owned by foreigners were a real problem. He was always getting pulled over for the most obscure reasons and of course a bribe was expected each time. He decided it was more trouble than it was worth and sold it. It took forever to get all the paperwork to be able to sell it but when he finally did, it was one of his happiest moments.

Moscow had twelve metro lines with 182 stations. There was a line around the inner city like a ring and then lines that went across.

Back when it was built, people had to have permission to live in Moscow and it was limited to a certain number of people and everybody had to have internal passports. Because of this, the metro was mainly used by the elite and was built as a showcase.

All the stations had individual character, and some were very beautiful. The closer to the city center, the more elaborate they became. For example, Revolutionary Square station was right off of Red Square and was full of marble statues. I had two favorites. One was Novoslobodskaya, which had thirty-two stained glass panels designed by Latvian artists. The other was Mayakovskaya, with thirty-four mosaics by Alexander Deyneka set into domes in the ceiling with the theme "Twenty-four Hour Soviet Sky." I loved to just go there and look up to see the amazing Soviet visions: "Bathers Jump in the Water," "Parachutists," and "Airplanes over the Kremlin."

We bought monthly passes for transportation (just a card with the month on it) which let me ride on anything: metro, trolley, bus, or tram. I mostly used the metro but sometimes I would catch a trolley-bus. The only problem was there was no set schedule so you could wait a long time for a bus and it could be very crowded when it arrived. The metro was more reliable but no less crowded.

Some of the escalators went really fast. It was great most of the time but it did have it drawbacks. Every once in a while, I would see a woman trying to extract her long fur coat from the bottom of the escalator. One day I was lucky enough to get on the escalator behind a woman who clearly had no brains. She put her trolley cart on the escalator in front of her with the wheels grounded in the back. When she got to the bottom, of course it got stuck and she could not push it off. All this time the escalator was continuing to move so I plowed into her while she was struggling with her bag and then people plowed into me from behind. What a nightmare!

I never felt scared or threatened walking around Moscow. Sometimes I felt confused and uncertain about what was going on, but I was never robbed or attacked. There were only two things that did scare me. If I saw a BMW parked on the street, I would usually cross the street right away. The Russian mafia were always putting out hits on each other and I did not want to get caught in the crossfire. But the thing that scared me the most was that a drunk would throw up on me in the metro. There were so many drunks, it was hard to avoid them. And often I would see an empty metro car and think, Yay, I can sit down, only to find it stinking of vomit—it was empty for a reason.

THE BRITISH EMBASSY

When I had first arrived in Moscow, I would check the bulletin board at the US Embassy. One day I saw an ad for a position at the British Embassy. I called them up and went in for an interview. This was 1993, and there were still very few expats in Moscow. The first man I met had lived in Nigeria so we hit it off. The embassy had just purchased a Windows computer and needed somebody to learn how to use it and to type letters, do formatting, and transcribe dictation for them. I could type and I had played around a bit on MS Windows so they hired me on the spot. Nicholas was not too thrilled because they did not pay much, but I was excited to have a job.

My first pay from the Brits was all in five-dollar bills. What a wad I came home with! I felt very rich and now we had money for groceries at the hard currency stores and any extra went to pay our American Express credit card bill at their Moscow office.

I enjoyed working with the Brits. In some ways I think I felt more comfortable with them than the Americans since they immediately grasped my sense of humor (which was sarcastic). The British Embassy was on the river, directly opposite the Kremlin in an old beautiful mansion. Apparently, it was owned by a Sugar Baron before the revolution and then it was confiscated by the state. The Brits were the first to have representation in Moscow, so I suppose that's why they got it. The inside was not huge, but the rooms were like palace rooms with high ceilings, gold on the woodwork, and inlaid parquet floors. Each room was a different color and the ambassador's sitting room had a huge carved wooden fireplace.

As beautiful as it was, however, I did not work there. The Commercial Department was in a separate building on the other side of town. I would get a ride in the morning from one of Nicholas's drivers and then I would take the metro home.

Soon after I started, I went to a reception at the British Embassy and met Anne, the Princess Royal and her new husband, Commander Laurence. We all stood in groups (essentially assigned clumps) in a semicircle and the commander and the ambassador's wife (who was an American) started at one side, Princess Anne and the ambassador started at the other so they spent about two or three minutes talking to each group. The commander seemed a little nervous but he was nice. Anne had on a bright green straight silk skirt and a fuchsia silk top. She carried a black silk purse with matching shoes and sported long white gloves. She was prettier in person than in her pictures and was very relaxed and charming. We drank Pimm's out on the lawn and it was lovely.

I worked at the British Embassy for about two years. When Nicholas went to work for the United States Information Service (USIS), he needed somebody to oversee the contracts he had with his newly formed translation and desktop publishing company. Then I left my job at the embassy and took over at the "family business."

The same week I changed jobs we went to the Bolshoi Theater. The Queen of England and President Boris Yeltsin of Russia were in attendance. We had aisle seats in the fourteenth row and we could see everything perfectly. The ballet was *Giselle*, and it was danced beautifully. Even Nicholas commented on how good the dancing was. And we could see the queen and Yeltsin come and go and wave. Before the ballet started, we were in the bar having a glass of Champagne with the Brits; one of them was very involved with the visit. He told us that the queen's dress had been locked in a room in the Kremlin (where she was staying) and nobody could find a key to the room. They were all panicking and calling the airport to see if they could get a replacement in time and finally somebody found a key and saved the day. When we saw her come out into the theater Nicholas said, "No wonder they locked the door." He was not impressed with her dress. For all the excitement, our tickets only cost seven dollars apiece—such a deal.

POLITICAL UNREST

In August 1993 I sent an email to my parents:

> I have been listening to the BBC all day telling me there is a diphtheria epidemic going on in Moscow. And the news the other night said somebody came down with cholera. So, maybe it's time to see about getting some shots.
>
> Boris Yeltsin has thrown down the gauntlet again and said if the Supreme Soviet doesn't hold elections this fall, he will. That should be interesting.
>
> Victor (our friend from Novosibirsk) was over for dinner the other night. He is a journalist so the government had brought him here for some convention. He was telling us that there used to be key words that caused immediate breaks in your connection when you were talking on the phone. For example, if you were talking to somebody and said "collaborate" the phone immediately went dead. He said the worst part of it was that people got so used to it happening.
>
> Everybody seems to be pretty discouraged with the way things are going but when I ask them what ideas they have that would make things better they never have any answers. They don't like Boris but there is nobody else that they do like.
>
> Oh well, interesting times.

In October 1993, Boris Yeltsin dissolved the Supreme Soviet and called for elections in December. The vice president, Rutskoy, declared himself president of Russia because he said what Boris did was illegal. So Rutskoy and the speaker, Khasbulatov, holed up in the parliament building (the Russian White House) with a bunch of their supporters. Yeltsin sent in troops to seal them off and gave them a deadline to hand over their weapons.

My office was right across the river from the White House. Troops moved in and blocked off the whole area. Streets were blocked off everywhere and I had trouble getting to work. Our driver said there were armed personnel carriers at the edge of the city. All kinds of rumors were flying around. The soldiers surrounding the White House looked bored to death and cold; we had had our first snowfall that week.

The majority of people in Moscow just ignored the whole thing. For them, it was business as usual. The really important problem of the day was that metro prices were going up and it was impossible to buy an October pass; they were only selling one token at a time, so the lines were horribly long at all the stations.

On Thursday troops were stationed in and around the city. Yeltsin announced on Friday that he would give the people in the White House until Monday to surrender their arms. On Saturday, there was a large demonstration just at the end of the Old Arbat not far from the White House.

On Sunday, Nicholas went to work and I stayed home and cleaned the house and read. I did not turn on the radio or TV all day. Nicholas came home at about 7 PM and said things were very bad. Demonstrators had marched from over by Gorky Park down the Garden Ring Road to the White House and broken through the barriers. Rutskoy—the "second president"—told the crowds to storm the mayoral building next door and take over Ostankino Tower, which was the main TV center.

We immediately turned on the TV to see a reporter saying he did not know how much longer he would be able to be on the air and that the building was under attack. Moments later the picture was gone. The Moscow channel was still on, but they were broadcasting from a backup station somewhere outside the city. We stayed up most of the night watching that channel and drinking vodka like every other Muscovite surely was. At some point the station reported that tanks were on their way to Ostankino—the beginning of the end. Gunfire went on until 6 AM but the government troops finally secured Ostankino. Sixty people died there. All stations were back on the air by midmorning.

Later that day tanks rolled into the city and surrounded the White House. I stayed home from work and sat glued to the TV all day. I am sure anybody watching CNN that day saw what I saw, but one thing they might have missed was Nicholas running across the bridge with his buddies taking pictures. He was out there about noon for about an hour. When I recognized him, I still could not believe my eyes. He said he saw two dead bodies about forty feet from him who were killed by snipers. Amazingly the crowds were out as if on a Sunday stroll. There were women all dressed up to the hilt parading down the bridge and children daring each other to be closest to the action.

The tanks fired on the White House and they arrested Rutskoy and Khasbulatov at about 5:30 PM along with a couple hundred people who surrendered around that time. Nicholas came home about 7:30 and there was some pretty gruesome footage of Ostankino from the night before on the news. Yeltsin announced a curfew starting at 11 PM and going until 5 AM to be in effect all week.

On Tuesday morning, the roads were still blocked all around my house so we took the metro. When I got to my office I went out onto Kutuzovsky Street to take a look and there were still tanks blocking the bridge and troops across the street. The White House was now more black than white. It burned through most of the night and the top half was all black and charred with soot. The building next door, which housed the mayor's office, was also badly damaged and burned out.

On Wednesday morning, our driver told us that 123 gunmen had been arrested around the city the previous evening. A man who worked for Nicholas and lived in an apartment across from the mayor's building had left home on Sunday and did not go back until Tuesday. When he returned, he found bullets all over his floor and embedded in his walls and his windows had been shot out. He spent part of the night sleeping under the bed.

Yeltsin gave a long speech on TV. He was really mad—you could tell. The bear's nose had been tweaked. It was a good speech but nobody knew what would happen next. He proclaimed a day of mourning for all the dead and there were new Russian flags flying down the street next to the White House. He also called off the honor guard that had guarded Lenin's tomb for decades in an apparent symbolic break with the past.

The Brits were blasé about everything as usual. They were all at work on Monday but they lived in the same building they worked in. They said the building had shaken every time the tanks fired.

TYPICAL MOSCOW LIFE

Moscow had a centralized heating system and hot water came into the apartment in pipes from one of the heating plants. Every summer these plants as well as the pipes needed maintenance, so they would turn off the hot water in different areas of the city at different times; consequently, we would go three to eight weeks without hot water depending on where we lived. It was a pain because I had to heat the water in the electric kettle for a bath and for dishes. I would take a plastic bucket and fill it with boiling water from the kettle and then put in some cold to the point where it was reasonable. Then I would take a cup and pour water over myself while standing in the bathtub. When I was growing up, we called it an Asian bath, since we always took baths that way in Burma. I could now relate to my mother who had lived in Burma for eight years without any hot water. Because the heat was centralized, in the winter the closer you lived to the plant, the warmer your apartment was. We would often have to keep a window open in winter because it was the only way of regulating the heat.

In Moscow, I came across a lot of contradictions. Some people were very interested in the West and were always asking about Western culture, history, and social issues. And some of them loved to draw similarities between Russia and the US by saying that we were very much alike. I wondered if these people were telling me what they thought I wanted to hear or if it was just that they had different backgrounds or what. I wondered if they were trained to work with foreigners. They seemed sincere and of course, there were some similarities. I just had a lot of trouble understanding these people and this country and, in some ways, could not relate. What exactly was their culture? Had the past seventy years had a serious impact on their culture? What did they have to fall back on? What did they believe in now? How could they become a democracy overnight? The country was having an identity crisis.

Another weird thing was that it snowed and snowed in Moscow but it never seemed to accumulate. It took me the longest time to figure it out. Big trucks came out at night that looked like giant crabs. They had two arms in the front that scooped all the snow into a feeder at the front and it went onto a conveyor belt that ended up getting dumped into another truck at the back. These trucks took the snow outside the city and dumped it into the countryside so there was never very much snow on the streets or sidewalks. What you ended up with was mainly ice, often black ice. I had many slips and falls because of it over the years.

One Sunday morning it was -15° C (-5 ° F) and the sun was out for the first time in a long time. I got up and walked across the park to the German Penta Hotel to get a Herald Tribune and some fresh croissants for breakfast. There were people jogging in the park and fresh snow on the ground. When I got to the lake I saw a guy standing on a bench with nothing on but a towel. He was just starting to get dressed after a dip in the lake. There was a big hole in the ice where he had apparently been. Russians also walked around Moscow eating ice cream no matter what the temperature was. I think it was Winston Churchill who said, "You cannot defeat a nation that enjoys ice cream at -40° C."

APARTMENT TWO

Even though I didn't want to move again, we had found a new apartment that was much airier than the old one. Plus Nicholas could have his own study to make his mess in. It was on the fourteenth floor and had a distant view of Red Square. It was farther from the metro but was also near a large park. The only problem was that the bathroom had ants that hung out around the faucets and there was no way to get rid of them.

People in Moscow would rent out their apartments for one year, sometimes two, and move in with relatives someplace else. They would charge high rent in hard currency to foreigners and save all the money and use it to renovate the apartment when they moved back in. We lived in six different apartments over nine years because the landladies kept kicking us out when they had saved enough to renovate.

The air seemed to be cleaner in our new apartment, and I could not see one smokestack nearby. At night we could look out the window and see St. Basil's and one of the Kremlin towers all lit up.

The second day there I filled up the kitchen sink to do the dishes. When I was done, I just pulled the plug, and all the water went rushing down the drain and came pouring out all over my feet. They had put new pipes in but when they met the old pipes, they did not fit together so they just rested the new pipe into the old one. When water came pouring out all at once, it got backed up and overflowed. We called the landlady, and she said she would call a plumber and come over the next day. Well, I came home the next evening and she had been here all right, and now there was a big rag neatly wrapped around the pipe! The Russians always had a practical way to "fix" things. Really, you had to laugh.

One morning Nicholas was working at home, and I left to go to work. I got into the lift and hit the button for the bottom floor. The lift moved in a jerky way. It felt like it was going up, then it stopped dead still. I was on the fourteenth floor. I began to freak out, shaking all over. I could see myself plummeting fourteen floors to my death. I hit the intercom button not expecting anything to happen. I hit it a couple of times, panicking. And then, I was amazed to hear a woman answer. She asked me what my address was. I told her (luckily, I knew enough Russian to be able to tell her). Somehow, I managed to get her to understand me. Pretty soon I heard somebody come to the landing. I yelled to them and they heard me. I told them to go get my husband and gave the apartment number (all in Russian). After a while, I heard Nicholas's voice. He said, "I'll be right back—I have to go get the video camera for this." Lovely. Such a funny guy.

Finally, after a long wait, a woman showed up, crawled in on top of the car and managed to get the door open. I was just below the landing and was able to crawl out. I was so happy and relieved. And it was all caught on video. I did not go to work that day. There was no way was I getting back into that lift.

SNAPSHOTS FROM RUSSIA

THE DACHA

Summers in Moscow were hot and humid. There was no air-conditioning, and the apartments were not built for warm weather. It was miserable. I used to plant myself directly in front of a fan and not move. Most people tried to get out of the city for at least part of the summer. In many cases dachas, or summer homes, were passed down from generation to generation. People grew vegetables, gathered mushrooms and berries, pickled and canned everything in sight, and returned to the city ready for winter. Generally, the dachas were small houses with a little garden for growing vegetables. The whole family shared the space. If they did not own a dacha, they could rent one or they could go to a rest house.

In Soviet times, people were assigned to rest houses based on the quality of their work, length of service, health, and other things. A committee existed in most factories to determine who would go. A rest house could range from a luxury hotel on the Black Sea to a few dorms in the woods where people shared communal jobs. Sochi on the Black Sea, for instance, was a favorite vacation spot.

We rented a dacha with Nicholas's cousin and family, in the small village of Petrovo-Dalneye, about an hour by car from Moscow. We rented the back half of a house where a woman lived year-round. She had a very large garden, two rabbit cages with about eight rabbits, and a bunch of chickens. We had two rooms, a kitchen, and a dining room and entry area off the kitchen. There was cold running water in the kitchen sink and that was it. You had to shoo away the chickens to get to the outhouse.

While there, we took the bus over to Arkhangelskoye, to the grounds of an old palace built in the eighteenth century that was under *remont* (renovation). It was in pretty bad shape at the time, but I heard it has since been restored and become a tourist attraction. It had a beautiful view and walking paths down to the Moscow River. We sat by the river for a while and got some sun. When we returned to the dacha, we ate dinner and then Nicholas and Valya went to the forest and picked mushrooms, which we later ate on a pizza. It was a pretty area, very rural with little vegetable gardens all over the place. I really enjoyed it and did not feel any particular need to return to Moscow.

ST. PETERSBURG

That same summer we flew up to St. Petersburg. First we took a taxi from the airport to the train station (part of the first railway built in Russia) and then took the *elektrichka* (electric train) out to Pushkin, formerly known as the Tsar's Village. There we were met by Nicholas's cousin Nellie's husband, Leonid, who took us to their apartment. Overall, it was quite the journey. They had a clean, fairly large apartment (two rooms—but big rooms) right next door to the Catherine Palace. Nicholas's Aunt Lolya lived with them. Her husband Nikolai had been a World War II hero who died in a plane crash in 1952, when he was just forty-four. There were originally five brothers: Michael, Alexander, Nikolai, Prokofiev, and Nicholas's father Vasily. Alexander lived in Moscow and we saw him from time to time and Nicholas's father lived in Milwaukee, but the other three had died long before I moved to Russia.

One afternoon we walked through the Catherine Palace and the accompanying gardens. All but one of the palaces in the area had been destroyed by the Germans, so they had been restored from fragments, drawings, or literary descriptions. Most of the rooms showed a photo of how each palace had looked before they restored it. It was clear that their former royal inhabitants had lived well. The rooms were overwhelming with gold all over the walls and beautifully inlaid floors. The gardens, bathhouses, little lakes, and bridges on the grounds went on and on.

The Catherine Palace was originally built for Peter the Great's wife, Catherine. The King of Prussia gave Peter the Amber Room as a present. The panels were shipped by boat to St. Petersburg and it eventually ended up in Catherine's Palace. The finished room contained 450 kilograms of amber. The room had been looted by the Germans during World War II and supposedly destroyed but nobody knows for sure what happened to it. From 1979 to 2003, Russian craftsmen worked to restore it with the help of German donations. The Amber Room is truly one of the wonders of the world. It was still a work-in-progress when I saw it but impressive, nonetheless.

At the Hermitage Museum in St. Petersburg, I saw Impressionists, Picasso's, some Da Vinci's, Rembrandt's, and beautiful rooms with portraits and mosaics. I also found room after room full of Matisse paintings. We spent about three hours walking around. From there we just walked along the river and through various parks—past the Field of Mars (named for the god of war) and down towards the Summer Palace, which was on the same street as the Winter Palace; they did not have far to travel.

Of course, there were tons of tourists and tour groups all over the place. Everywhere we went they had a different admission price for Russians and for foreigners. At the Hermitage it was 400 rubles for Russians and 7,000 rubles for foreigners. Nicholas's cousins bought all the tickets for us so we went in as Russians everywhere and I was told to keep my mouth shut when entering places. The only place we had a problem was at the Hermitage—the woman spotted us as foreigners and started asking me questions in Russian. At this point Nicholas whipped out his journalist accreditation and claimed immunity, so I showed her my ID card, and after some more yelling she let us through. His cousins were appalled at the difference in price.

We also went to the Pavlovsk Palace (named after Catherine the Great's son), which was not too far from where we were staying. It was not quite as lavish as the Catherine Palace, but it was known for its collection of clocks, and the huge garden and forest that surrounded it. It had a park with all kinds of statues hidden away inside it. There was one avenue lined solely with birch trees that were already starting to change a little, so it was very colorful.

BORODINO

Another memorable trip was when our friend Leyna's husband got a company car and we drove to Borodino. Borodino was where the battle of 1812 against Napoleon was fought and the inspiration for the *1812 Overture*. There was a small museum with a model showing where all the soldiers had been positioned for the battle. Borodino was made up of fields and forest with little towns interspersed and monuments scattered throughout. There was a beautiful nunnery on the grounds that also had monuments with sections of the trenches and fortifications from the battle. We drove all over the area and then picnicked under some trees where we ourselves became lunch for a large number of mosquitoes.

It was a beautiful day—warm in the sun with a cool breeze. I could not believe that such a nice place existed in Russia. There were wildflowers growing and mounds of harvested hay dotting the area. Birch trees lined the road. Getting out of Moscow always improved my general view of Russia.

Almost twenty years after I had seen the *1812 Overture* performed on the esplanade in Boston, I found myself at another outdoor concert, in Red Square, Moscow. It was winter and the square was jammed with people. We were all smooshed together, keeping each other warm. The conductor, a Russian, had been living in exile and this was his first concert after being welcomed back. The newspaper commemorated the occasion: "Washington Chorus Society and USA National Symphony Orchestra, conducted by Mstislav Rostropovich, perform the finale of Prokofiev's Cantata *Alexander Nevsky* and Tchaikovsky's *1812 Overture* with Kremlin Cathedral Bells and Cannon Volleys."

Both the concert in Boston on the Fourth of July all those years ago and this one in Moscow were significant events. On that beautiful day in Borodino it dawned on me that the *1812 Overture* was a strange way to celebrate the Fourth of July. Tchaikovsky wrote it to celebrate Russia's defense of Moscow against Napoleon at Borodino. And now I had been to the fields of Borodino where that final battle was fought. I guess since it was such a great piece of music, it did not matter where it came from.

MY FAVORITE PLACES

The statue of Yuri Gagarin in Moscow is so cool. In 1961, he was the first human to go into space. The monument is made of titanium, and he looks like a comic book hero. It always made me think of Astro Boy, one of my favorite cartoon heroes.

Then there's the story of St. Basil's on Red Square, built in the mid-1500s. Ivan the Terrible commissioned an architect to build the most beautiful church possible. So, the architect did what was asked of him. And then Ivan the Terrible (who did not have that name for nothing) ordered the architect to be blinded so he could not create anything so beautiful again. It is probably a myth, but every time I came up the street onto Red Square it took my breath away. If you could be there at night when it was snowing, you were lucky indeed.

Another one of my favorites was the Exhibition of Achievements of the National Economy, or Vystavka Dostizheniy Narodnogo Khozyaystva (VDNKh). At the entrance to the VDNKh exhibition grounds was the famous statue of the two farm workers with the sickle and the wheat. As you entered the gates, the Friendship of People fountain was in front of you, bright, shiny, gold, and happy looking. There were large exhibition halls promoting things for sale that were always changing. But the fun part was at the very end of the park where they had a Tupolev Tu-154 airplane as well as several others that you could go into. Stalin originally built the exhibition grounds to glorify communism, but to me it was just a fun place to go. It also had a big amusement park and there was a small *Space Pavilion*, which were both great places to take kids. My son had his first donkey ride in that park.

APARTMENT THREE

The landlady kicked us out of our apartment number two because she found out that Nicholas was running a business out of it and since it was not technically legal, she freaked out. This meant we not only had to find a new apartment but an office as well. Nicholas had lost the job he had with the American company and decided to start his own translation and desktop publishing business just to tide him over until he could find another job.

We took an office in a nice area that was too big for us and too expensive, but we were in a position where we needed something right away. Nicholas seemed to think we would grow into it and that maybe we would be able to justify staying there. We placed an ad to hire another person. Then we got a new contract to translate fourteen more technical manuals we needed to hire some more people. The building was all offices except for a shoe wholesaler on the first floor. We were in one big room with a wooden floor and murals of mountains and rivers on the walls. It was very Soviet, glorifying nature and the people of the USSR. We were only about two blocks from the metro, so it was convenient.

By "Soviet" I mean a certain style. The Soviets built big ugly concrete buildings, with no frills. The art was mostly propaganda and often oversized: large figures doing things together to glorify the State or help the People. Or pictures of wheat fields, agricultural prosperity, and modern machinery. All the people looked kind of robotic and everything was exaggerated.

We were on the first floor and the women's toilets were on the third. The place was pretty disgusting. I took my own toilet paper but only one stall had a seat cover on the bowl. This meant that if it was taken, I had to squat over the toilet to pee, which was not easy. Most of the public toilets in Russia (at least the ones I encountered) were either pots without seats on them which meant you had to squat over a toilet—which really made no sense—or you were in an outhouse. In many cases the outhouse was preferable. There was also the occasional hole in the floor, squat situation as well. All in all, it was not pleasant. I could never figure out how a country with a space program could not put together a decent bathroom.

We also signed a year's lease on a new apartment. It was a smaller and more expensive place—two rooms instead of three—but the rooms were large, and the location was perfect. It was in an elite building with a concierge (a babushka who looked at you funny when you walked in). One of our neighbors was a famous rock singer, Alla Pugacheva, who always had fans holding vigils outside. The apartment had beautiful parquet floors and was clean. It was on the ninth floor, so the view was good and it was up off the street, but not so far to walk down to the ground floor if necessary.

One night we were shaken out of bed in the middle of the night. I thought it was an earthquake, but it kept going and going so then I thought we were being invaded. I looked out the window and there were these huge tanks rolling down the middle of our street in the middle of the night. What was going on? It turns out they were practicing for the big military parades on Victory Day.

The following week was the fiftieth anniversary celebration of World War II VE Day. We took the video camera and went down to Red Square where there were big banners waving like flags around a large stage. We watched the Hare Krishnas chanting and placing a wreath on the Tomb of the Unknown Soldier which was very surreal. On May 9 we celebrated without having to leave our apartment. First, we watched the parade broadcast from Red Square on TV. Then the

Communists paraded down our street waving red flags and carrying pictures of Lenin and Stalin. Next, the military parade came down our street under our balcony, tanks ripping up the road. Then later in the day the marching bands paraded down our street. And in the middle of all the marching bands was the McFarland High School Band from Wisconsin playing "On, Wisconsin!" Unbelievable.

Around this time, Nicholas and I had some kind of rebirth where we started to get along really well. Actually, we had never gotten along better. I got pregnant in the middle of November. I was happy about having a little baby. I went from being scared to death to being elated. I started taking Russian lessons again. It did not look like I would ever get out of Russia. Nicholas said a year and a half more and that was all, but I did not believe it.

I was quite sick the first few months of my pregnancy. I had quit smoking when I turned thirty, but I had had several relapses and would still smoke occasionally when out drinking. Once morning sickness hit, however, that was the end of my cigarette romance. I could not even stand the smell. Luckily none of Nicholas's relatives smoked; and even though a lot of Russians smoked, they never did in other people's houses, they always stepped outside, so that helped.

I planned to leave in June to go to Minnesota to wait for the baby's arrival (in August) and then I was to return sometime in September. Nicholas had insisted the child be born in the US so he or she could be president one day, if he or she wanted to. I thought this was kind of silly, but I was happy to go home and not deal with any Russian hospitals.

I knew it was important that Nicholas and I continued to grow in our relationship so that we could be good parents. I started to read *The Tibetan Book of Living and Dying*. I needed to get back in touch with my spiritual side so if new issues in our relationship did come up, I could just let them go instead of having them consume me. Inside I knew my husband loved me very much and that I loved my husband. It was really amazing to see how our love had grown over the years and changed. We had some kind of connection, something beyond his confused outer self. It was nothing I could really explain. I knew inside him there was something truly good. And little by little it was presenting itself. The more I focused on the positive, the more I felt my life would just get better and better.

I was wallowing in all these warm and fuzzy hallucinations about my husband when we hit a wall. He became consumed with another woman. Our marriage was possibly over, the business was needing more attention, and he became embroiled in a huge political scenario with work. Her boss knew about their relationship, I knew about it, probably everybody knew about it. I was pretty sure my baby knew about it. I worried that my son would be affected somehow by it all. I hoped he would not be a sad person his whole life because I was so sad during my pregnancy. He certainly was an active little monster. He kicked me all the time.

I arrived in the US on June 21, after spending five days in Amsterdam. Emotionally I was a mess. I tried to pretend that everything was okay with Nicholas but it was not. Things were pretty bad. I was beginning to seriously doubt if I would be returning to Moscow. Being pregnant intensified everything; I felt that the only reason to stay with Nicholas was for the baby's sake and I just did not know if that was enough.

Ultimately I was who I was, and I could not change that; there really was nothing I could do about the situation. All I could do at this point was ride it out, see what would happen, and try to prepare myself as best I could for every outcome.

APARTMENT FOUR

My son, Noah, was seven weeks old when he and I boarded the flight back to Moscow from Minnesota. I said a teary-eyed goodbye to my family, unsure I wanted to leave but not feeling like I had a lot of options. Noah was a good traveler and I actually got a round of applause from my fellow passengers as we deplaned and people stopped to tell me what a good baby he was. When we finally arrived in Moscow, we were ushered to the head of the line at passport control and breezed through customs. Nicholas was not there. He showed up about ten minutes later saying he had gotten a flat tire.

So, we got a taxi to the tire repair shop and waited for it to be fixed and then went home.

The apartment was a horrible mess with boxes everywhere. We had been kicked out of our last apartment mainly because our one-year lease was up but also because we had moved some of their books that they left in the living room. They did not want us to touch any of their stuff, so it was on to apartment number four.

The new apartment was out in the suburbs about a thirty-minute metro ride into town. The air was cleaner and it was quiet with a big park nearby. It had almost no furniture so we had to sleep on the floor until we were able to buy a bed. There were a couple of chairs in the living room. Luckily, there were armoires so we could at least unpack stuff. I spent the first three days doing nothing but unpacking and taking care of Noah. It finally got to a point where I could tolerate the place.

In March, my visa was due for renewal, so Noah and I went to Finland to visit a friend of mine. We stayed on the coast in Vaasa for the weekend where we drank wine in her tiny apartment, walked in the winter wonderland, and watched wind surfers on the ice. It was a wonderful, marvelous break and so refreshing to have somebody to talk to. Nicholas's girlfriend had dumped him, so things were a bit strange at home. While he was moping around, I wrote an email to the woman and told her what I thought of her and the damage she had done. I know it takes two, but I have zero respect for people who become involved with married men or women. What the hell? Bitch. If he was really in love, why didn't he leave me? For some reason he never did. He kept coming home. But after this experience, I lost much of my trust and respect for him. Why did I stay? Because I did not have an exit strategy, I had a child to take care of—and because I'm a survivor.

I breast-fed Noah for six months and then switched to formula when I had to go back to work. I found one that did not make him sick and managed to get a regular supply at the children's department store, Detsky Mir. After a few months they ran out. I went to every store I could think of looking for formula. Sometimes I could find it at a kiosk on the street. I was then forced to switch to a different brand and hoped he could tolerate it, and he did, but then that brand disappeared as well. We did make it through until he went off of formula but there were times when I thought I would have to beg somebody to ship me some.

I'm sure some of you are thinking: Formula? Ugh. She could have made her own or pumped. At the time though I had plenty of other problems to deal with, so it just was not an option. But Noah survived and grew into a healthy child—a large, healthy child. I used cloth diapers until he grew out of them and then I switched to paper. In fact, he got so big I had trouble finding diapers to fit him. I went through the same drill as with the formula, hitting up every store I could think of.

Finally, I connected with a woman who knew of a place where I could get extra-large diapers. She gave me an address in an apartment block. The entrance was around the back and downstairs in the basement. A very large man in a leather coat guarded the door. I felt like a criminal. Inside was a large room with a man sitting at a small desk in the entranceway. Boxes of diapers were piled high in the back. He had what I was looking for and I bought a large box to keep me going for a while. Sometimes he would be out and I would either have to go back on the prowl or buy a smaller size. The potty training phase did not come soon enough. By the time we left Moscow six years later, I could have purchased any type of formula and any size diaper I wanted easily. My timing was off.

When I went back to work part-time, our landlady's mother, Ida, lived in the building next door and she agreed to stay with Noah while I was at work. She was a grandmother who stayed with us until we left Moscow six years later. Noah was in love with her, and I think she fell in love with him. It was like having family around.

APARTMENT FIVE

After another year, we were on the move again. Apartment number five was within walking distance of the US Embassy and very close to the center of town. It had been nice to be out of the city for a while but now it was good to be back. There were two metro stations I could walk to and a big grocery store around the corner. The apartment was pretty nice. It had two bedrooms, a good-sized kitchen, and a large living room with big bay windows. At the same time it could have used some renovations; there was horrible wallpaper, old windows, a separate bath and toilet, overly large wall units, and an overall drab look, but it was a step up from the last one. We already had a pretty good bed and we bought a couch and a chair so we did not have to sit on the floor anymore.

I decided to stick it out in Moscow. I was content at work and enjoyed my child. I had grown a lot in the past couple of years, and I was beginning to understand some things about myself and about how my life could be. I saw a lot of possibilities and my outlook was good. I was already a survivor of many unpleasant things and I knew I could be happy again. The answer to happiness was not to be found in other people but deep within myself. Other women would not make Nicholas whole, just as I was not able to. He had to find the missing piece inside himself, just as he could not fully satisfy me and my needs. I had to figure out how to do that myself and make things happen the way I wanted them to. At the moment things were pretty good. I hoped they would become better.

Then in November Nicholas lost his latest consulting job, and he could not find any steady work. We basically ran out of money and were living day-to-day, unsure if we should stay or go back to the States. Time trudged on. Our business did not do a damn thing for three months. We just sat there twiddling our thumbs and reading the overdue bill notices. In April, the wind changed—we actually started making money and had our best month ever. May was not as good but we still made money, so we decided to give it to the fall to see if things continued.

That summer was very hot. Aunt Lolya died in St. Petersburg and Nicholas and his cousins Lev and Valery went up on the train to help with the cremation. When Nicholas got back, he said that because of the heat, there had been a record number of deaths and they had to put all the bodies in one big room with no refrigeration. His aunt had been dead about three days by the time they could claim the body and have it cremated. I'm glad I was not there.

Later in the year Nellie and her husband, Leonid, brought the ashes down and we buried them next to her husband, Uncle Nikolay. We all got together that day over at cousin Raisa's house and had a big meal and drank a lot of vodka. Uncle Shura's wife, Yelena, got drunk and passed out and then she woke up argumentative which kind of put a damper on things. That's how things usually were at Nicholas's family gatherings.

Our family business was doing pretty well. We were translating technical manuals and delivering them formatted the same way we received them. We had several newsletters we translated and had printed on a regular basis and new business was coming in. Then one day the general director quit on the spot. We did not understand it at the time; we thought maybe she had flipped out or something since she had been a loyal employee for four years. Several of her friends had helped us along the way, among them our lawyer, our landlord, and our editor. After she left, the lawyer would not work with us, the landlord kicked us out so we had to find a new and ultimately more expensive office space, and our editor all of a sudden had other commitments. Then we found out that our director who quit had set up a competing business in our old office space and taken four of our employees with her. This, of course, was the price of doing business but it seemed like it happened often in Russia. It was all a big blow to us both emotionally and financially and Nicholas in particular was furious.

With the 1998 financial crisis and the devaluation of the ruble, more difficulties emerged because the bank we had been using for the business was in serious trouble and froze our account. Even when they unfroze it, the money in the bank was worth about half of what it was worth before. We also had people who owed us large sums of money and it looked like they would not be able to pay us back.

Things were not the greatest for us, but we did still have clients, and work was coming in and there was still a potential for some large accounts. We were in better shape than a lot of people. The aisles at the grocery stores became a bit bare and rumor had it that the supply of imported goods had dried up. One morning one of our employees saw a tin of coffee for sale for 50 rubles. The next afternoon it was on sale for 75 rubles. Everybody was scrambling to find dollars as the ruble was worthless and nobody wanted it, but it was very difficult to get dollars. The exchange places and ATMs were not giving them out.

People were not panicking yet; they seemed to be able to keep their sense of humor about it all. Nobody knew what would happen next. All kinds of rumors were flying around like reports of tanks outside the city. After all, this was Russia and anything could happen—and it usually did. My impression was that most people thought things would straighten themselves out eventually. There was really nothing to be done about it at that moment.

AMERICAN WOMEN

I had joined the American Women's Organization (AWO) in Moscow soon after I arrived. I ended up not getting too involved because the women who ran it were not very friendly to me. Half of them thought my husband was Russian and therefore inferior to their American husbands—even though he was not Russian, but that was a mere technicality. They organized shopping trips and took tours. I worked full time. They lived in big, beautiful renovated apartments and had drivers. I was out of their league, not that I wanted to be in it, I was just hoping to make some friends. My mother said she never joined those organizations because they were too political. Somebody always wanted to boss everybody else around. I could see her point, but I had joined because I felt so isolated and wanted to be accepted.

The AWO did some good things for us, though. They put on a Halloween party every year so Noah could get dressed up and actually go someplace. They sponsored a Christmas party every year at the US Ambassador's residence, which is where I met Lizzy. She had just arrived in Moscow and was stuffing Christmas cookies into her jacket pocket. She said they were to take home to her children since she did not know where to shop to find ingredients to make cookies. So I invited her over to make cookies at my house.

Lizzy ended up volunteering to work on the AWO newsletter. She needed some help with her computer one day and asked me to come over to give her a hand. We became friends but she was only in Moscow for one year; when she left, she handed over all her newsletter stuff to me and asked if I would do it. It seemed simple enough so I took it over. I quite enjoyed it because it was a creative outlet and it kept me in the loop with everything that was going on.

When Nicholas and I had first gotten together, he had filled my small condo in Minneapolis with his stuff and his big personality. I responded by retreating to the kitchen. It was the only place that was truly mine and I made sure it stayed that way. I had been a casual cook before, but once I finally arrived in Moscow, I took on a new identity: Kathy the chef.

There were no convenience foods available when I first arrived in Moscow. I made everything from scratch. Corn tortillas, wheat tortillas, and tomato salsa, all to make enchiladas and tacos. I made multiple varieties of lasagna with and without meat, quiches with homemade crust, eggplant parmesan, soufflé, ratatouille, Fettuccine Alfredo, pasta primavera, and peanut curry. These were all specialties of mine. I had learned from my mother that recipes were only guidelines. When living in places where items might be hard to find, learning the art of substitution was critical. I made pancake syrup with Sprite and maple flavoring. My son still reminisces about it. I perfected making fruit pies and cream pies and I baked intricate cakes, all with whatever ingredients I could find at the time.

I had plenty of people to use as my guinea pigs. Over time Nicholas invited what seemed like half the population of Moscow over for dinner—and they all came. I joined an expat group of six couples that took turns cooking for each other once a month. The hostess came up with a theme and everybody brought a dish. It was a creative outlet and a good way to meet new people.

I do not remember how it happened but at some point, I decided it would be a good idea to make a cookbook for the American Women's Organization in Moscow. I started to solicit recipes through the newsletter and at meetings. After a while everybody knew me and some women even became friendly towards me. We formed a cookbook committee to work on the format and do research. We ended up producing a very good cookbook with all kinds of reference information like conversion tables, substitutions, and where to find things in Moscow. It was a big success and sold out. I did not make a ton of friends, but I felt better about myself.

TOTAL ECLIPSE OF THE SUN

In order to continue to live in Moscow we had to renew our visas every year. This always meant having an AIDS test and leaving the country to reenter with the new visa. It was a good excuse for a vacation. Over the years I renewed my visa in Holland, Finland, Italy, and France. In 1999, there was a total eclipse of the sun in Western Europe, so we decided to combine our visa renewal with a visit to old friends living in Paris and watch the eclipse.

We decided that Metz, France would be a good place to view the eclipse. We rented a car and drove from Paris to Metz, stopping on our way to see the cathedral in Reims with its stained-glass windows designed by Chagall (who was born a Russian). Once in Metz, we scoped out the area and early the next morning we headed out with the telescope, video camera, and other cameras. We set up our camp in the middle of the esplanade, which was a nice park right by the river. The town had organized a big festival around the eclipse and so there were parades and music going on all day long.

The weather turned out to be cloudy. During the first half of the eclipse, we were able to see it off and on, but about twenty minutes before total eclipse it started to rain. We could tell when the total was, though, because it was completely dark. All the flowers closed up and all the lights came on and it was really night and kind of eerie. Then during the second half it cleared up a bit and we were able to see more. Four-year-old Noah kept looking at the eclipsed sun through his glasses and referring to it as the moon. Nicholas got some good shots through his telescope, and I got a new umbrella. When we returned to Paris, our friends who had gone twenty-five minutes north of Paris on the train said they had seen the whole thing perfectly.

From Metz we drove south towards the Vosges area. We stopped at the Haut-Koenigsbourg castle, which was a restored castle on top of a mountain in the middle of the forest. From that vantage, we could see forever. It had a moat, a drawbridge, and an inner yard. It would have been very hard to penetrate. We hiked up to it and since it had been raining the path was muddy. I commented on how mucky it was and Noah asked, "Monkeys? Where are the monkeys?" He would not let it go.

We wound our way down the road to La Bresse, which was in the heart of a big ski area amid mountains and forest. We hiked around a glacial pool; Noah spent the better part of an hour throwing rocks into it and hunting for dragonflies.

Back in Paris we stayed with our friends who had lived in Moscow and had a child Noah's age. Joseph and Noah had been best friends in Moscow. We all spent a day on the rides in one of Paris's many parks and did some sightseeing. On our last day in Paris we had lunch up at Montmartre with all the tourists in town.

After we returned to Moscow, one night Noah was in bed going to sleep and he asked me if we had been to America. I said no. He said, "Oh, no, no we were in Caris." No, I said, you mean France. He said, "No, not France, Caris." I said, "You mean Paris?" He said, "Yes, Paris. That's where Joseph lives." He was a slightly confused four-year-old world traveler.

APARTMENT SIX

We lasted for two years in apartment number five. The landlord ended up selling the apartment and kicking us out with about two weeks' notice. What a nice guy. Luckily, we had already been looking elsewhere and were about to sign a lease. Apartment number six was just down the street from number five, but it was much nicer. It had been remodeled and had an all-in-one Western-style bathroom and the apartment was big and airy, which I loved. We had bought a Western refrigerator (twice the size of our usual Russian ones) and the apartment came with a washer and dryer; it was amazing, almost like living in a civilized country. There was even room to set up a jungle gym in Noah's room. Most Russian children had some kind of jungle gym inside—it helped when you had six months of winter.

This was also the first apartment that was not infested with cockroaches. We had time to fumigate before we moved in and they did a good job. Up until then every apartment had been a cockroach hotel. Going into the kitchen at night and switching on the lights made my stomach turn. They would scatter but I always knew they were there. I gave up trying to kill them. I tried to coexist—although I guess it was more like blocking it out. Moscow had rats, too. I never saw them in the apartment, but I often saw them on the street.

Nicholas was back running the family business and frankly it was difficult to live and work together so I applied for a job at the US Embassy. The US Embassy allowed Americans living in Moscow to join their club for a fee. This included a pool, a gym, showers, a video rental store, and the cafeteria. We belonged to the club the whole time we lived there so I was very familiar with the compound. The embassy was a strange place. It was a large compound with one multistoried building, an older Russian building that looked like a palace but was originally built as an apartment building, the recreational complex, and then two streets lined with townhouses and apartments with a large green area in the middle. Everything was surrounded by a high wall with two guard gates with US Marines checking everybody as they came and went. The cars were all checked with mirrors underneath. But with its clean and perfectly manicured streets, it was like being in the suburban US. I think some people never left the compound. It had a fairly large commissary, but we were not allowed to use it.

The multistoried building was built by the Russians and when the Americans moved in, they found millions of surveillance bugs. So, they tore down the top floor and added on two stories of their own. That was the secured area with the safe rooms and top-secret info. I enjoyed going to the embassy because, besides the pool and video rentals, I could have a hot shower whenever the city turned off my hot water at home.

I started work at the US Embassy's consular section in October of 1999. The first day sixty of us went to the embassy's dacha and had training on American Citizen Services. This was because they were preparing for Y2K. Most people thought Y2K would basically be the end of the world. Microsoft and I guess other companies as well had set up their computers to only use two digits to represent the year. That worked fine as long as it was 19XX. Moving to 20XX meant only having two digits could be a problem and everybody was afraid that the computers would get all confused and stop working. Since everything was connected to computers, it could have been a real disaster—no water, no electricity, no heat, airplanes falling out of the sky, and trains stopping abruptly.

In order to deal with all the Americans in Moscow, everybody at the embassy needed to be ready in case there was a disaster. I thought they were probably blowing everything out of proportion, but they felt they had to be ready for anything. They planned for the possible evacuation of the 20,000 US citizens registered in Moscow and the surrounding areas.

NBC came and did a story on Nicholas, Noah, and me preparing for Y2K, stocking up on food and water and filling the bathtub with water. A reporter, cameraman, and soundman followed us around to various supermarkets (one of which would not allow them in) and then they came to our apartment and interviewed us. Noah, of course, was very interested in the camera. They said we would air New Year's Eve.

Of course, our TV debut was preempted by Boris Yeltsin resigning and the announcement of who his successor was: Vladimir Putin. That was a big shock to everybody. We knew right away things would change for everybody—and not in a good way.

BACK TO LUGANO

In the fall of 2000, we decided to put Noah into a Russian kindergarten. It was in our neighborhood so he would not have to travel by car and it seemed to be a nice one. Plus, it was affordable. We hoped the change would not be too traumatic for him. Russian had been his first language, and he understood absolutely every word but had refused to speak any Russian after we returned from our last trip to the US. He was not thrilled with the school, but I hoped he would warm up to it.

One great thing about living overseas was being exposed to different cultures and traditions all the time. I figured Noah was young enough that even if he did not get a lot out of Russian school he certainly would get something out of living in Moscow and meeting lots of different people and traveling around Europe.

Before school started, it was again time to renew our visas. The founder of The American School in Switzerland (TASIS) where I went to high school was to celebrate her ninetieth birthday that year so we decided to spend a few days in Lugano via Milan.

We flew to Milan on Aeroflot. It was a brand-new Airbus and somehow we ended up in first class, which was a much more pleasant experience than my first Aeroflot trip to Helsinki back in 1991. In Milan we had some nice relaxing meals and did some sightseeing. When we went to get our visas, one disturbing thing happened; they called Nicholas in to "interview" him. They had never done that before and we were a little uncomfortable about it. This was the start of the

Putin era and we knew things were beginning to change. But they did give us our visas in the end. We spent most of the day at the Leonardo da Vinci Science and Technology Museum, which Noah really loved because they had whole trains, planes, and even a huge sailing ship in there. We soon discovered, however, that Milan was not the best place to be. Most places were closed in August because everybody had gone off on vacation. We kept running into dead ends, so we hopped on a train and spent five glorious days in Lugano, Switzerland, on the lake surrounded by mountains, one of the most beautiful places on earth.

The weather was hot and sunny. We took the funiculars up two mountains, hiked around, and even had a picnic in a meadow I used to hike to as a student. We rented a motorboat and drove around the lake and Noah went swimming. For Nicholas's birthday we had dinner at Capo San Martino, which hangs cliff-side over the lake just outside of town.

On the weekend we headed up to TASIS for Mrs. Fleming's ninetieth birthday celebration. Some of my dear friends were there—two old roommates and an old boyfriend. We hiked up to see Herman Hesse's old house. Now there was a small museum next door dedicated to him. We looked around for our old stomping grounds; we found out that the hole in the wall where Serafina served us wine and beer out of her own kitchen was now closed, but the main restaurant in the small village of Montagnola was still there. We spent a pleasant afternoon sipping grappa the owner had made himself. He even sold us several bottles.

Unfortunately, Nicholas, Noah, and I had to get back to Milan to catch our flight back to Moscow, so we could not stay for the banquet, but we had a great time anyway. Noah cried when we left because he really liked my school and made several friends—I practically did not see him for two days because he was off playing with his new friends. He was like a typical Third Culture Kid, finding that home is wherever you are.

Eleven years later I went back to Switzerland with Noah as a teenager. Mamma Fleming died at the age of ninety-eight and was buried in the cemetery just down the mountain from the school, where Herman Hesse's grave could also be found.

In the years since my last visit, the place had changed dramatically. Lugano was still as beautiful as ever although much more built up and congested. The piazza was full of tourists but the pizza was still good. The local department store where we had purchased my son his Action Man toy in 2000 was still there but had a new name and was under new ownership.

I almost did not recognize the school because there were so many new buildings. It had become a formal school with students in uniforms and actual rules. When I went there it was very much a family atmosphere with a hodgepodge of buildings and living arrangements. I think I liked it better the way it was before—rustic and inviting.

NEW YEAR'S RESOLUTION

Back in Moscow, we knew it was winter because it was so dark. However, the mayor did a good job that year, and every store window was decorated and lights were everywhere. There were strands of white lights looped all along one of the main shopping streets and several buildings were completely covered in lights. I took a stroll along Red Square, looking beautiful with the fresh snowfall. Then I walked through GUM, the big department store, and I had never seen such an assortment of Christmas paraphernalia outside of the US. Every kind of decoration you could imagine was for sale. I even heard "Jingle Bells" playing over the loudspeaker in the metro. I thought I had lost my mind. But such was life in Russia—you never knew what would happen next.

After all my years in Russia, I finally came to understand what bothered me. It was that life had a cheapness to it. Most foreigners who lived in Russia saw a generous, attentive, and friendly people. Russians would go to any lengths to help you with any problem. They would listen to you and tell you anecdotes about their lives that paralleled yours. They would tell you anything they thought you wanted to hear, and somehow or other they would get whatever it was they were looking for from you. In most cases, you would find that these people were most friendly and generous when they were on your payroll. Some of these folks were Russian teachers, drivers, cleaning ladies, nannies, secretaries, or salespeople. They all managed to creep into your lives. I think most foreigners left thinking they had a very good experience and loved the Russian people. And because the Russians were so good at illusion, they were probably correct. They did have a good experience.

When our general director quit after four years with us, I spent a lot of time looking back over those four years and all the time we had spent together. We entertained each other in our homes, we had been through personal joy and hardship together, and our families had even spent a weekend in the countryside together.

In retrospect, I realized that she had been telling me lies for four years. What I thought were coincidental contradictions were blatant lies. She told me whatever it took for me to put my trust in her so she could get what she wanted, even up to the day she quit. She picked a fight with me that day in front of the whole team and got me riled up. And then she quit. She used me beautifully, and I felt like a royal fool.

It made me look at other people I had known over the years and wonder about things they had told me. Unfortunately, it made me start to look at everybody (and everything) differently.

I noticed that the apartment buildings were an illustration of society at large. The common areas were dirty, run-down, defaced, and ugly. Often there would be no light because somebody had stolen the light bulb to use in their apartment. The buttons on the lift would be melted from vandalism. Yet, when you entered an apartment, it was neat and clean and even luxurious in some cases. People did not respect each other or care. Other people did not matter, only your own life did. It all came down to one thing: life was cheap.

Of course, I did meet people who were intelligent and kind and I had many good experiences and made some good friends. However, my original thought in 1993, that Russia was having an identity crisis, had changed. I now believed they were so used to being told what to do and how to live that many of them, especially the older ones, were unable to adjust or change. A lot of things changed in the 1990s but really, fundamentally, not much had changed.

My New Year's resolution for 2001 became: It was time to leave.

THE QUICK EXIT

After eight years, I decided I would not spend another winter in the Land of Darkness. In April 2001, I applied for a job with the US Foreign Service. I figured if they hired me at least they would send me someplace else and it would be an easy way to move on and still have a job. Nicholas said he would come with me, but I really did not care if he did or not. This was my exit strategy.

It was a long process but I finally got an interview in August. I was accepted but I still had to go through a top-secret security check and medical exam. So, going into the fall, we continued to wait. But then came the terrorist attacks in New York and Washington, D.C., affecting everybody in the world.

On September 11, I was just about to leave work when somebody came rushing into the room and said, "Quick, turn on the TV." We turned it on and saw a plane fly into the World Trade Center in New York. We all looked at each other. What was it? An accident? Slowly it dawned on us what was happening. This was the second tower to be hit. Nobody really knew exactly what was going on but it occurred to me that I was standing in a US Embassy and it might not have been the best place to be at the time. I hightailed it out of there. I spent the evening and subsequent days glued to CNN.

It was interesting to see the amount of flowers, candles, icons, and other things that were left in front of the US Embassy in Moscow. It was mostly Russians who came to give their condolences but I had

American friends who did not know where else to go so they, too, went and left flowers outside the US Embassy. The expatriate community came together in small groups to talk about their feelings and process.

About two weeks after the September 11 attacks something happened that was to drastically change our lives. Two men showed up at Nicholas's office and identified themselves as Federal Security Service (FSB) officers. These people used to be known as the KGB; they were not nice people. They asked Nicholas a lot of questions about his work and what he was doing in Russia. They asked him about his visa and then they asked him if his wife worked. At that moment he knew what they wanted. He thought about not answering them but he knew they already had the answers to all the questions they were asking so he decided to be honest with them. "My wife works at the US Embassy," he said.

The FSB wanted Nicholas to spy for them. They wanted information about people at the embassy. They wanted to know who had weaknesses and bad habits. They could use this information to then blackmail people into providing sensitive information to the Russians. People thought this kind of thing did not happen anymore, but it still happened, believe me. They were very clear about what they wanted and mentioned that they could "make things easier" for Nicholas in Russia if he cooperated.

Nicholas tried to stall them and told them he would have to think about it. He was told that if he went to the US Embassy and reported their visit, they would have to deport him. He was also told to obviously not mention anything to his wife. They agreed to meet the next morning to hear his decision.

The next morning Nicholas went to the US Embassy and reported the visit to the security officer. He did not go to the previously agreed upon meeting. Later in the morning he received a phone call on his cell phone from one of the FSB agents, even though he never gave them his cell phone number. The agent asked why he did not show up at the meeting. Nicholas said he had decided against working for them. The agent was angry and said that now he could do nothing for Nicholas and he would get deported.

My husband called me up and said we needed to have lunch. I could tell something was wrong and on the way to lunch I was trying to imagine the worst. I did not even come close. I went back to my office and started to explain matters to my supervisors. Most people did not think anything would come of it. They thought that maybe the FSB had tried and failed and now it would just go away. Or they might try again but nobody really took it too seriously. They said things like, "This is not the Soviet Union anymore, they cannot do that," or "You should get a lawyer and fight this, this is not legal." I had certainly lived in Russia long enough to know that it did not really matter if it was legal or not and that the state could do whatever it wanted to do.

I had seen Edmond Pope fight for almost a year to get out of jail for buying something that was available on the Internet yet somebody had decided it was "classified" information. He was sentenced to twenty years in prison for spying. I had seen the FSB accuse Fulbright Scholar John Tobin of being a spy and frame him with drugs. He spent several months in jail probably for the same reason my husband was facing deportation. This all happened while I was working at the embassy. We became cautious and waited to see what would happen next.

Two weeks went by and nothing happened. We started to think that maybe we were overreacting and that nothing would happen after all.

In order to get a Russian visa, you needed an invitation from a registered company or an individual. If you went as a tourist, it was easy to get an invitation from a hotel or a travel agency and when you arrived, you registered with the hotel or the travel agency. Most tourist visas were for no more than one month. Business visas were a bit trickier to obtain; you needed a letter of invitation from the company you would be working for. This company in turn had to have permission from the government to invite people. In order to get permission, the company had to be registered with the government in a certain way and pay certain fees. Then the government gave them one or two or however many slots that they could use to invite people over. If they needed more people, it was just too bad.

My husband's company was not registered in such a way that he could invite people over, so he had to get his visa though other sources. For this reason, there were lots of visa agencies in Moscow. These people specialized in matching companies that had slots they did not need with people who needed visas. People bought the invitation from the company and then took that invitation to the Russian Consulate in another country and were issued a visa. Then when they arrived in Moscow they went to the Ministry of the Interior and registered themselves as working for the company that issued the invitation. This was common practice. Because there was a shortage of slots, even several of the large law firms in town had to get their visas this way. Probably about half of the expats in town used this process. My husband had lived in Moscow for ten years on visas like this and never had a problem.

On Wednesday, the visa agency called and asked Nicholas if he had been having any problems with his visa. Nicholas said he would go to their office and tell them about it. The people from the agency were called in to speak with the Ministry of the Interior. The next day the head of the company that issued the invitation for Nicholas was called in.

This man was told to write a letter indicating that my husband's services were no longer needed. He was told exactly what to write. On Friday, Nicholas got a call from the Ministry of the Interior and was told that he should come down to their offices with his wife on Monday morning. We knew what this meant, so we told the people at the embassy where we were going and who we were going to talk to. I was scared we would be arrested but Nicholas was sure they would not do anything to us.

The FSB agents had told Nicholas that once we were deported we would have ten days to leave the country, so at 9:30 Monday morning we showed up at the ministry ready for that possibility. We were told that we had to sign sworn statements. They took us into a drab room with no windows. The walls were blank and dirty with the requisite grey-green paint. The air was musty with three big desks and two men sitting at the desks, smoking. There was one big black telephone on one of the desks and nothing else except for the forms to be filled out by hand (there were no computers). The conversation was only in Russian. One of the men asked us if we understood why we were there. My husband said he very clearly understood—it was because he had refused to spy for the FSB. I started to panic. How could he be such an asshole and provoke them directly like that? The man behind the desk did not blink. The black phone rang right on cue. I could not believe it. I was living in the middle of a le Carré spy novel.

The official picked up the phone without saying a word, listened for a while, and replaced the receiver. He then said, "Okay, I will have to write that down." My husband said, "Fine," and he wrote it down. Panic ran through me. What did that mean?

The ministry official also had the letter from the company saying that Nicholas no longer worked for them and so added that to the statement saying that there was no reason for Nicholas to remain in Moscow since his services were no longer needed by the company that had issued his invitation.

As for me, all my statement said was that I would leave because my husband was leaving. My visa was through a different company so they did not have anything on me at the time and probably were not that interested in me. At this point we found out we were not being deported. Instead, our visas were being cancelled. We were told we had ten days to leave from the day the ministry had received the letter from the company. Since they had received the letter the previous Thursday, we had until Friday to leave the country. This was Monday—four days. That was it. If we did not leave on Friday, we would be deported.

We were told to wait for the supervisor to come and make the final decision on our case; we waited for two hours. The final decision was that my husband had no reason to stay in Moscow because the company he was working for no longer needed his services. Paragraph two said that the Moscow FSB office had requested that he be removed from the country. Mine just said that I would be accompanying my husband. Our son was never mentioned.

I worked on Tuesday. I packed and sorted through nine years of accumulated belongings on Wednesday and Thursday. We left on Friday with six suitcases.

The hardest thing we had to do was say goodbye to Ida, Noah's nanny. We all cried. I held my breath as we went through customs and waited to board the plane. Once we were airborne, I let out a big sigh of relief. Goodbye, Russia.

PART SIX

THE AFTERMATH 2001

We had had to borrow money to buy our plane tickets out of Moscow. Now we had no place to go, no jobs, and only six suitcases. We were essentially refugees in our own country. We flew to Wisconsin and stayed with my parents for a couple of weeks, but they had just moved to a retirement home in Madison and we could not stay there long-term. My oldest brother was living in Northfield, Minnesota and offered to put us up in his basement. After a couple of weeks of that, we found an apartment about a block away for pretty cheap and he furnished it. I was very lucky because my father helped us pay for our apartment and my other brother loaned us a car. Both Nicholas and I sent out resume after resume but received not even a nibble. It was still soon after the 9/11 attacks and nobody was interested in people who had been out of the country for nine years. At least nobody in Minnesota was interested.

I was still waiting for my top-secret clearance from the US State Department. They lost my file for two months until I finally found somebody who agreed to go over there and ask about it. After that, a government security agent came to see me a couple of times to ask questions. He told me that even if I was cleared, I would have to go in front of a panel because of the "incident." I assumed this meant they would need to question me further and evaluate me based on the circumstances surrounding our leaving Russia. Since Nicholas and I had reported it immediately, I felt we had done everything we could to make it clear we were not spies. In the end I had been forced to give up my job, my personal belongings, my home, everything, because of this. What more could I have done? I found it insulting that I was being put under such scrutiny. I decided to withdraw my application.

Since I was in the US, I no longer needed an exit strategy. I would have liked to work for the US Foreign Service and continue to travel the world but it was now not as important to me and I had other options. I could speak English and my family was nearby to support me. I had old friends in the neighborhood, so I just needed to push through the disappointment and move on.

We enrolled Noah in first grade since he was six. After two weeks his teacher called me in to tell me he was not adjusting well and he was not really mature enough to be in the first grade. His English was not very good either. Apparently, his time in Russian school had mixed him up a bit. They were very nice about it all and ended up finding him a spot in all-day kindergarten which he liked.

I think I was in shock that whole first year. It felt like my life was foggy, distant, and unreal. After being away for so long, I would go into a store like Target or the grocery store; there were so many things and so many different kinds of the same item, that I would get sensory overload, unable to process what I saw, just standing frozen in the middle of the store. Seriously how do you decide what kind of tinned tomatoes you should buy? Does it make any difference? Is one better? Which one? Or orange juice? There's pulp, no pulp, calcium, extra pulp, from concentrate and on and on .... After a while I would leave without buying anything.

I interviewed for a job with the city and the man ended up telling me I could have access to the food bank if I needed it. I realized I must have sounded pretty desperate. I managed to find some temporary jobs. I had one job at a trucking company where I opened envelopes full of receipts and scanned them. Some of the receipts were all sticky and disgusting. I had about a forty-five-minute drive to work and I would cry all the way home. After a while I landed a job at GE doing data entry, which was much nicer. I rarely spoke to anybody but I listened to what people in the cubicles around me said. One day I heard a woman say, "I don't care if they take away my rights as long as they keep me safe." It made me cringe. Post 9/11 America was a strange place.

After a while, we managed to get a few of our boxes out of Russia but we had to leave most of our things there. Awhile after the whole US State Department job fell apart, we decided we had to look elsewhere for work. Within two weeks, Nicholas had found a job in Washington, D.C. He left right away to look for a place to live. He had only been there a week when his father died. All five brothers were now dead. We met in Milwaukee for the funeral and then I went back to Northfield to pack. We drove a U-Haul full of the furniture my brother had given me and our meager belongings cross-country to D.C. Nicholas found a townhouse in northern Virginia. We moved in on the hottest day of the year. We still had some things I had put in storage when I first moved to Moscow, so we had most of what we needed. And within a few weeks I was offered a good job in the IT department of a nonprofit.

ANOTHER NEW PLACE

Adjusting to life back in the US was difficult. I had been though reverse culture shock once before so I knew what it was like. Even so, because of the circumstances of our arrival, I was in pretty severe shock for a while. I honestly do not remember a lot of it. I'm lucky to have such a supportive family. I managed to get through it and make the move to Washington, D.C. where things started to become more or less normal.

My son experienced his first culture shock. He was now six and had lived in Russia his entire life. When we visited the US, we saw relatives and did not spend a lot of time wandering around. We were focused on seeing everybody and getting shopping done. After moving, Noah started noticing that America was not the clean and perfect place he had always thought it was. He started asking questions about all the homeless people. He was happy to be with family but sometimes had trouble relating to his peers. It took some adjusting.

In first grade his class was doing "Christmas Songs Around the World" and when they came to Germany he said, "That's where the Nazis were." He was always interested in history, and World War II was something he knew a lot about because his Russian grandfather had been a POW in Germany. None of the kids in his class knew what he was talking about and his teacher reprimanded him for mentioning it. He did not know why. He could not understand why Americans did not know world history or geography. Even in middle school he would complain that the kids in his class thought the Nazis came from Russia.

He would talk about places he had been, or knew about, and his peers did not know anything about them.

When we first moved to northern Virginia we lived in a suburb where the children at Noah's school were almost all white. I think there was one family from Africa. I had trouble figuring out PTA meetings and coping with all the politics of public schools. Most of the people thought I was strange and were not friendly. I decided I didn't want my son growing up in such a place. So halfway through the sixth grade we moved to Falls Church, on the Arlington border. This was a much more diverse area with many immigrants and people of color. He was not too happy to move at the time, but I think it was better for him in the long run. He made some very good TCK friends.

Back when I was living in Russia, I toyed with the idea of writing a book and I came up with a title I liked: *Global Nomad*. I went looking on the Internet to see if somebody had already used that title and came across a website for Global Nomads International. There was an article written by Norma McCaig, the founder. I could not believe what I was reading. This woman knew what I knew, felt what I felt, lived what I lived. She got it. I had plenty of friends who got it, too but we never talked about a whole subculture or a label. I had now been labeled. I was a Global Nomad because I had grown up outside my passport country because of my father's work.

This article opened up a whole new world for me. I found other writings and research on the Internet. I even hooked up with a woman in California, Ann Baker Cottrell, who was soliciting information for research she was doing. I learned about Dr. Ruth Hill Useem who coined the term Third Culture Kids. I read everything I could find on the subject.

I had exchanged a few emails with Norma McCaig and I knew she lived nearby so I looked her up when we settled in Virginia. We attended several gatherings at her house and when she organized a Global Nomads Conference in 2003, I offered to help and played a very small role. The conference was a great success and there I met Ann

Baker Cottrell and Ruth Van Reken. Ruth was selling a book she had co-authored with David Pollock titled, *Third Culture Kids: Growing Up Among Worlds* so I bought it. I call it the TCK bible. It tells you everything you need to know. I recommend it to everybody, it's been such an important book to me.

MOVING ON

It's funny where the winding path of life can take you. The curves, the detours, the gentle hills, and the sheer drop-offs. When there's nothing else to do but to scale back up and take a new turn. Sometimes I look back on the things I have done and wonder how I ever managed to do them. In the midst of living life, one just slogs through somehow and then later looks back thinking, Wow, how did I muster the courage to do that?

After Nicholas's affair during my pregnancy, my feelings for him changed. I no longer thought things would get better or change. I resolved myself to the way things were and given my circumstances, I carved out a life for myself in Moscow and then in Virginia. I started to write and journal more. I tried to be a good mother, and I had very low expectations for my marriage.

Nicholas's job in Washington was working with Russians on exchange programs. He started to slip back into his old habits of staying out late, drinking, and spending time with other women. I did not pay too much attention.

In the spring of 2004, I realized I could be on my own again and I was not afraid. I had a good job that paid well, and it was enough to support me and my child. I hoped Nicholas would help with child support, but I figured I could manage either way. All the infidelity had taken a toll on me, and I was finally able to accept that I was not a failure and there was nothing wrong with me. I had done my best and tried my hardest but it was clear, Nicholas and I were just not meant to be. The thing was, at this point our marriage was not terrible; it just was not much of anything at all. I felt like I had a roommate who I spent time with occasionally but did not really communicate with and could not trust. I decided there had to be more to life and I deserved to be happy—or at least to give it a try.

I did not expect the reaction we got when we told Noah that we were separating. He cried and cried. In my warped state, his reaction was something I did not foresee. In a way, that was a good thing because had I been more aware, I might not have been able to go through with it, for the sake of him.

Divorce meant once again letting go, splitting up possessions, and starting over. I went through a major downsizing where I let go of most of my possessions. I kept some things I really liked but mostly it just did not matter to me. As a single mom I put my energy into raising my child and making a living. I worked long hours and made good money. I became a loner.

Then in April of 2011, Nicholas had a seizure at work. They found a tumor in his brain and after it was removed, they determined it was an aggressive form of brain cancer, stage four. With the help of chemo, he lived a pretty normal life for the next year. He had a very positive outlook throughout his illness, but then the chemo stopped working.

Nicholas had tried to go back to Russia soon after our departure. It was five years before they would give him a visa. He had been back once but his dream was to go back with Noah now that he was a bit older. They had planned to go in the spring of 2013 but in August 2012, the trip was moved up and they went for a two-week visit. They saw relatives, friends, and many of their old stomping grounds. It was a dream come true for both of them.

A few weeks after they returned, Nicholas was admitted to the hospital with rolling seizures. They tried several drugs and he was able to recover up to a point. They gave him several different treatments to shrink the tumors but they just kept spreading. In December, he was told to seek hospice.

By this time, Nicholas had a girlfriend living with him. She was about fifteen years younger than him (he was fifty-eight) and in complete denial about Nicholas's condition. She tried to make everything seem normal all the time. This really bothered Noah. He finally told me he did not want to go over there alone and asked me to go with him. So, I went. It was very weird. I understood why Noah did not want to go. Nicholas was a different person. He sat and watched old reruns on TV all day and seemed to really enjoy it. He had always loved movies, but TV? Not so much. He really was not himself anymore. And the girlfriend was pushing for them to be a "happy family."

Things took a turn for the worse and the girlfriend alerted Nicholas's sisters and Noah that they should come. One of his sisters flew out and Noah and I met her at the apartment. Nicholas was in a coma, or at least was not responsive. We spent four days sitting with him, giving him morphine, reading to him, talking—watching him die.

I had trouble understanding why this had happened. It seemed so random. I searched the Internet to learn more about brain tumors and brain cancer. No one seemed to know why it happened. What caused it? There was one unproven theory that cell phones were the cause and Nicholas was an early adopter of the mobile phone but it was just a theory. Where did it come from? Was it genetic? Environmental? The luck of the draw? All of the above? We know how people get smallpox or cholera. But brain tumors? I know a few people who have since died of brain tumors. It seems to be more common than I thought. Apparently, it is the sixth most common cause of cancer-related death among people over forty, with glioblastoma (the kind he had) making up 16% of those.

He died on January 17, 2013. It was all very sad. I did not expect to have such a strong reaction. It hit me pretty hard. We had thirty years of memories together. I still dream about him.

MY LAST MOVE?

"In the end, many TCKs develop a migratory instinct that controls their lives. Along with their chronic rootlessness is a feeling of restlessness: "Here, where I am today, is temporary. But as soon as I finish my schooling, get a job, or purchase a home, I'll settle down." Somehow the settling down never quite happens. The present is never enough—something always seems lacking. An unrealistic attachment to the past, or a persistent expectation that the next place will finally be home, can lead to this inner restlessness that keeps the TCK always moving."

–Ruth Van Reken and David Pollock, *Third Culture Kids*

I had finished school, gotten a good job, purchased a home, and had a child. I was settled down. Or was I?

I rearranged the furniture. I planned long elaborate trips all over the world. I poured over airline timetables. I read travelogues.

I lived in Russia for many years with the landlady's furniture or no furniture at all. It drove me crazy. I would complain to my husband, "When are we going to be able to buy some decent furniture that is comfortable and just be in one place for a while?" I dreamed of living in a comfortable place that was my own where I could *relax*.

I still dreamed about it. It was always someplace cozy and small and it was raining outside. But the truth is, I hate the rain. I find it confining.

I reread *Hidden Immigrants* by Linda Bell. In this book she interviewed people like me who grew up overseas, constantly moving around. In one section she explores roots. Most of us are not joiners. We do not get really involved with local communities. We do not identify with place. Where we are is always temporary. Our roots are in our friends and family. She writes:

> What ties do they feel are important as they enter mid-life?
>
> The answer is people—friends, and often old friends… For it is those old friendships that validate their childhood, reaffirm those places for them and tell them something about who they were at that time. People are real —better than pictures, better than memories. Even if they only connect with these people once a year, or see them very occasionally at school reunions, or write or call them infrequently, these connections are the bedrock of their past.

I guess I was having my own flavor of midlife crisis. My roots were not in northern Virginia or Washington, D.C. I needed a change and a new adventure.

A year after Nicholas died, Noah graduated from high school. I had lived in the area for twelve years, longer than I had lived anywhere. The few friends I had either moved away or were moving. There was nothing to keep me in the area so I started thinking of what to do next. I had started traveling again and had been to Canada and to Europe a couple of times and to Florida with my high school friends. I was getting reacquainted with them and it was like no time had passed. We were still as close as ever.

I had a good job working in the IT Department of a nonprofit as their business manager, doing the budget, procurement, and software management. It paid well, but I was tired of it and my new boss picked on me. The commute was getting worse by the day. I was ready to move on.

My parents were getting older and slower and had just moved to Minnesota to be closer to my brothers. My son was going to college in Minnesota. Minnesota seemed like the place to be. I decided to quit my job, pack up my stuff, and move to St. Paul. Back to the deep freeze.

I had a beautiful condo in Falls Church, Virginia with a large porch that looked onto some trees. Cardinals, jay birds, mourning doves, and other birds lived in my trees. They could be very loud but I enjoyed them. On one lovely sunny fall day, I was sitting on my porch having my morning coffee and I thought, Will I miss this? Will I miss my porch and my view? Will I? Have I ever actually missed anyplace?

It was hard to leave places but the hard part was really saying goodbye to friends. I lost a lot of things along the way like dolls, toys, records, books, and clothes. But I never missed them the way I missed the people. It was not the city, the house, or the things. When I arrived at my new home in my new city I never wished I was back where I had come from.

The reality was I could not go back. The unique set of circumstances that made up my life in that moment would not be the same. Everything would have changed. The city, the people, the house. The experience would be different. After leaving Mexico I went back a couple of times to visit to find that my neighbors had moved, my friends had moved on, and the city had grown. I saw some familiar sites but I was now a tourist. The whole dynamic had changed.

I had left Minnesota twenty-five years earlier. Since then, I had lived in Florida, Washington, D.C., Moscow, and Virginia. I had lived in twelve different apartments. I did not miss any of them. I saw this particular move as going back to the future. I did not expect it to be anything like my previous life in Minnesota. I would be learning about a new place and meeting new people. Some of it would be familiar but much of it would not be. I did not expect it to nor did I want it to be.

When I had first moved to Minnesota back in the 1980s, I did not know anything about Third Culture Kids. I was fresh out of college, having a difficult time adapting to my passport country. I did not understand why people reacted to me the way they did. When I went for job interviews in Minneapolis, I thought I would bring something special to the table. I clearly could get along with all kinds of people, was well-educated, and was smart. But when the interview was over, they would ask, "Are you going to finally settle down and stay in one place for a while?" I did not understand the question. What difference did it make?

As I adjusted to Minnesota culture back in the 1980s, I realized that it was another foreign country to me. Most people had lived there their whole lives and few had done much traveling. Although it was a progressive state, many people were conservative. I learned to bury my past even deeper and watched a lot of TV so I would have something to talk to people about.

Since then, Minnesota had become more diverse. There had been a large influx of refugees. Minnesota now has one of the highest numbers of refugees per capita of any state. Also, now I was armed with the fact that I knew much more about myself. I knew how to use my past to an advantage without scaring people off. My new strategy was to not disclose much about myself at first. Once I got to know somebody a little, then I would tell them about a few places I had lived or visited. People seemed to be able to take my stories in small doses. I liked to try and tell them about other places, cultures, people, and traditions in a low-key way and maybe not even saying anything about myself. That seemed to work pretty well. It made me feel good to broaden someone else's mind if I could.

I knew I would still be different and there would be people who thought I was odd but it did not bother me. I was comfortable with who I was. Plus, I had lived in the same place for the past twelve years so that showed that I could stick it out. Starting over at my age would never be easy, but who said life was easy? I thought, Yes, I might miss my sunny porch on dark winter days ... but then again, maybe not.

AFTERWORD: THE TRAVELS CONTINUE

I have been settled in my new home now for ten years, but I still travel as much as possible. That is my new normal. Even so, traveling these days makes me nervous. I get a stomachache, worry about getting to the airport on time, and pack weeks in advance. Hey, I'm a seasoned traveler. I should have it all down, no problem—but no. I still don't like to fly although airports are like a second home. I can sit in an airport for hours and never get bored. I would probably be more relaxed if I just stayed in one place. A lot of people do it—many for generations.

Looking back, I've had a pretty unique life. I have learned that a lot of expats and TCKs lived in one country or two. Many of them were missionaries who tended to stay in one country. Some were business or diplomat families who had incredible support systems including their own health clinics, doctors, and security teams. There are many, many different stories. According to the World Population Review website, there were more than eight million expats living overseas in 2024. Life overseas has changed since I was a child. The world is much smaller. Communications have improved. Facebook has made it easy to connect with and stay in touch with old friends. There has been an effort to educate people about the unique issues TCKs and expats face. I'm not sure it is easier, but it is less traumatic when you know you are not alone and what to expect.

Somebody told me they thought I probably had PTSD. Therapists who work with TCKs have written a lot on this subject. Yes, I had some traumatic experiences, and I have a few triggers, but I honestly do not feel scarred. I loved growing up and traveling all over the world and meeting all the interesting people I came into contact with. I always made an effort to stay in touch with friends and I tried to bring people together. And the thing is, I really never knew anything different. I will probably always be rootless and restless. It is like the grief and the guilt—it's just something I live with.

I hear over and over again how people are searching for home. Where is home? Home is where you feel comfortable. I went to a Rainbow Gathering many years ago. The Rainbow Tribe was a group of people who met once a year in remote forests to celebrate peace and all live together in harmony, no matter who you were. When I arrived in a remote area of the North Carolina Smoky Mountains, there were people who greeted me and showed me where to go and how to get around. They all said, "Welcome home." I was so impressed by that. I knew exactly what they meant. "Welcome to a gathering of like-minded people. Our tribe." And once I discovered I actually had a tribe of my own, it made even more sense.

Many people do seek help through therapy to make sense of their strange lives. From what I have read it can be difficult to find a therapist who actually understands the unique problems TCKs have. I recently read *Incredible Lives and the Courage to Live Them* by the British therapist Dr. Rachel Cason. I found it helpful and real without getting too deep into the professional mumbo jumbo.

Dr. Cason writes:

> Our stories are real. They are our Truths, and we are the authority on them. But often the significance of our experiences has been blurred, put out of focus, by a lack of shared perspective with those around us. For many, including TCKs, even close family members have vastly different accounts and experiences of childhood mem-

ories and cultural identities. All this can contribute to a sense of un-reality, a blurriness about our Selves, a lack of confidence in our own Story.

For our stories to feel real, they must become tangible. How can our histories be experienced in the now, carried into the future, and shared with new witnesses, if they remain invisible and intangible? We need tangible objects that can represent our histories and our Selves, especially when walking, talking witnesses to our lives are lacking. These objects are the "identity props."

My house if full of "identity props." I have elephant bells from Burma, wall hangings and carvings from Africa, nesting dolls from Russia, and pictures from Mexico. Things my parents had in their home and things I acquired myself. All are part of my story.

My parents are both gone now. They lived long full lives. I see my brothers fairly often but we have different memories. We share some but many we do not, and we have different perspectives. There really is not anybody around who bears witness to my whole story. I do have friends and relatives who have shared segments of it though and that is comforting.

My son grew up living overseas and traveling. My husband and I took him everywhere. He developed this incredible ability to sleep anywhere, through anything. He is now a second-generation TCK with a strong desire to travel the world.

When I started to write this book, I was overwhelmed by emotion after emotion. I would spend whole chapters crying over my keyboard. I did not really understand it but it became such an incredible release that I had to keep going. Everything came pouring out. One thing we are told over and over again is we have to tell our stories. Whether it is to a therapist, to a blog, to a friend, to a relative, to the great beyond, or whatever. We just need to tell them, to get them out.

Thank you for reading mine.

USHUAIA, ARGENTINA 2017

In 1984, I went to Spain. I boarded a train in Granada headed for Seville. My ticket had a seat number on it but I could not find the seat in the car I was assigned to. Confused, I asked a guy who was standing in the aisle. It turned out he was as confused as I was and could not find his seat either. After a fairly long conversation in Spanish, he asked me where I was from. It turned out he was a schoolteacher from Oregon. We decided to pick random seats and got to talking about places we had been and places we would like to go. I mentioned I wanted to see more of South America and he suggested I read *The Old Patagonian Express* by Paul Theroux. It was about a trip from Boston to Tierra del Fuego mostly by train. His description of the southernmost tip of the world left a big impression on me. It sounded beautiful, otherworldly, and almost eerie. A special place. I decided I had to go there. Thirty-three years later, I finally fulfilled my dream.

Tierra del Fuego is an island that sits at the southernmost tip of South America in Argentina. Ushuaia, its capital, is on the Beagle Channel about halfway between the Atlantic and Pacific Oceans, 620 miles from Antarctica. The meeting of the two oceans along with the mountainous terrain creates strange weather patterns. It was usually very windy and there could be rain, sun, and storms, all within the same hour. It never rained for long and usually not very heavily. It was more like mist than rain. One could be out walking in the rain and never feel wet.

As we flew into Ushuaia, I could tell the pilot was having to do some maneuvering, swooping down in-between the mountains to deal with the heavy winds. Once we hit the ground, I started to cry. It had taken me more than thirty years to get there but I was finally here. It was an amazing feeling. And the beauty of it did not disappoint; it was even more beautiful than I had imagined. The light and color were like nothing I had ever seen before. The area was dominated by snow-covered mountains all around. Before arriving, I had been worried that the excursions I had reserved would be cancelled because the weather forecast called for rain every day. I soon realized, rain meant nothing in Ushuaia. Life went on no matter what the weather was.

One of our tour guides said the only people carrying umbrellas in Ushuaia were tourists. Because of the winds, umbrellas were useless.

IRELAND 2019

Our first stop out of Dublin was Brú na Bóinne. This is a Neolithic period World Heritage Site comprised of Knowth, Newgrange, and Dowth. We spent three hours touring Knowth and Newgrange.

The highlight for me was Newgrange. It consisted of one large main mound built 5,000 years ago, before the pyramids of Egypt or Stonehenge in England. It was an incredible display of engineering. We were led into the mound for a demonstration of how the winter solstice lights up the cave-like structure. I am not a fan of small tight spaces and almost did not go in but luckily, we were not in there for very long, so I did not have time to panic.

Our next destination was Ballybay. This was the place my ancestors had listed as their home when they boarded the ship for America back in the late 1700s. Since I had spoken with a genealogist in Dublin, I knew they had probably not come from the town itself but the general area. I was really more interested in the countryside. The area was lovely with farms, sheep, rolling hills, and trees shading the road. We even spent some time sharing the road with a tractor.

A few days later we stopped at Kylemore Abbey in western Ireland. Originally built by a wealthy doctor from London for his wife, the abbey has been home to Benedictine nuns for one hundred years. The nuns ran a girl's boarding school from 1923 to 2010. They currently offer residential and day retreats. The grounds included a Gothic chapel and Victorian gardens.

We took a boat from Doolin to Inisheer Island, the closest of the three Aran Islands. It took about forty minutes. On the island we wandered around the ruins, the farmland, the town, and the coast. It was beautiful though kind of desolate. The islands were known for the Aran Sweater which is usually off-white in color with a cable design made of pure wool. We decided the sheep must live on the other side of the island because we did not see any.

EGYPT 2022

My son and I decided to go to Egypt towards the end of the Covid pandemic. The only Covid-related requirement for entry was proof of full vaccination. I needed to set up the proof with a QR code on my phone, which was easily done. Getting back into the US was a little more complicated, but more about that later.

After a couple of days sightseeing in Cairo, we got up at four in the morning to catch an early flight to Aswan where we checked in on our cruise ship and had some lunch. Our ship was called the MS Tulip. It had four floors and a top deck. There were only about forty of us so we got a lot of attention from the staff with a couple of them hovering over us at all meals. One of them said "bon appétit" whenever he took a plate away. The food was abundant and for the most part pretty good. After reading *Death on the Nile* by Agatha Christie many years ago, I had always wanted to float down the Nile. Though thankfully there was no murder this time….

The next day was another early day; we had to catch a flight to Abu Simbel. We flew down and back in one day. I was not very happy since we had to take a lot of planes, but it was worth it. Abu Simbel is 230 kilometers southwest of Aswan near the Sudanese border. It was a sunny day and the flight was spectacular. I never imagined the desert having such interesting terrain. Big black rock dominated with specks of green along the river. As we descended, we caught a glimpse of the temple from the air. It took my breath away. This ended up being the highlight of my trip, my dream come true.

As a young girl in Mexico, I had a very colorful history teacher who brought history to life. He told exciting detailed stories of Alexander the Great, Ramesses II, Queen Hatshepsut, and many others. One of his best stories was about the great temple that Ramesses II built into the mountain at the edge of the Nile River in 1200 BC. After learning about this magnificent temple at Abu Simbel, I read that the Aswan Dam was going to bury it underwater; this upset me because I wanted to go see it. In 1968, an international team of engineers successfully moved the temple 65 meters up and 200 meters back in order to save it. I was sad not to see the original but still excited nonetheless.

There were two temples at Abu Simbel. They sat next to each other against their artificial mountains. The Temple of King Ramesses II was the larger one with statues measuring 20 meters (66 ft) high. Above the statues were twenty-two baboons worshiping the rising sun. Inside there was a main hall and chambers off to the side with a sanctuary at the back. In the sanctuary were four seated figures: Ra-Horakhty (the sun god), King Ramesses, Amun-Ra (the creator of all things), and Ptah (god of craftsmen and architects).

The second temple was built for King Ramesses's wife, Queen Nefertari. The statues of the king and queen at its entrance are half the size at 10 meters (33 ft) high. It is rare in Egypt to see the queen depicted as the same size as the king, so it is clear she was important to him.

We returned to Aswan in the afternoon and as soon as we boarded our cruise ship, we set sail downriver. In Egypt up is down, as the river flows north to the Mediterranean. After dark, we stopped at Kom Ombo to visit the joint temple of Sobek (the crocodile god) and Horus (the falcon god), and the Crocodile Museum. The temple was built about 350 BC. It has been damaged by earthquakes, erosion, and builders stealing rock to build other things, but on a clear night with a full moon, it was beautiful.

We docked in Luxor at lunchtime and in the afternoon, we set out for the Temple of Karnak, built about 4,000 years ago. It was a large complex built for the priests and the king; no others were allowed entry. The entrance was lined with ram-headed sphinxes. As we entered, we saw the Great Hypostyle Hall which was 54,000 square feet with 134 massive columns all beautifully painted. All but twelve columns are 10 meters (33 ft) high with the remaining ones being 21 meters high (69 ft). The site is considered the largest religious building in the world.

By the time we left Karnak, it was getting dark, which is apparently the best time to see Luxor Temple. The temple was built about 1400 BC and was used mainly for coronations. In about 395 AD, the Romans occupied Egypt and converted the temple into a fortress and later put a Christian chapel inside. In 640 AD a mosque was added and is still used to this day. There were originally two obelisks at its entrance. One is now at the Place de la Concorde in Paris. Our guide kept lamenting how many things had been stolen from Egypt. Recently excavated and open to the public, the Avenue of the Sphinxes ran from Luxor Temple to Karnak, with 600 sphinxes and stretching 2000 meters long (1.24 miles).

The next day, it was about a half-hour drive from our ship to the Valley of the Kings. Only twelve of the sixty-three tombs that have been discovered are open to the public at any given time, and they are rotated as they are worked on and restored. We saw four of them. The whole area was still being actively excavated. Some tombs were in better shape than others. King Tutankhamun's tomb was the only one that still had a mummy in it and it was to be moved soon. It is hard to describe the experience, it was beyond beautiful and so amazing to think how old everything was.

I had read all the Amelia Peabody books by Egyptologist Barbara Mertz aka Elizabeth Peters that span the time from 1884-1923. She wrote twenty books based in Egypt mostly about archeologists digging around and solving mysteries. As I read them, I kept trying to imagine what the Valley of the Kings actually looked like back then, or even now. All I could imagine was a vast desert with nothing much else. Well, now I know: it was a hilly desert.

At Luxor we said goodbye to our cruise ship and flew back to Cairo.

Cairo, a city of over 20 million people, was big, noisy, smoggy, and dirty. But not as dirty as I expected. There were no open sewers, no piles of trash, and no stench. It was quite nice, really. On our last day we went out to Giza to see the Great Pyramid and the Sphinx. The Sphinx was smaller than I had imagined, but otherwise, my expectations were met. Fifty years earlier, my father had visited Egypt and went to Giza and rode a camel. I have a photo of him sitting on his camel in full Arab regalia. My father told Noah, my son, he should ride a camel, so we tried to recreate the same scene from the photo.

That morning on our way to Giza, we stopped in a parking lot across from the pyramids to rendezvous with a physician. He diligently swabbed all of us and went off to run our Covid tests. This was required for us to reenter the US. Later that afternoon I received an email with my official document, photo and all, proclaiming I did not have Covid. That was a relief. On the way out of Egypt, the airline did check to see I had the document but on returning to the US, nobody even mentioned it. All they looked at was my passport.

Egypt did not disappoint on any level. It was amazing.

LONGYEARBYEN, SVALBARD 2023

I had wanted to go to Longyearbyen in Svalbard, Norway, above the Arctic Circle. It is the northernmost city in the world. I had been to Ushuaia, the southernmost city and now I was going to the north. We started out in Aberdeen, Scotland and stopped in Fair Isle, Shetland; several towns in the Faroe Islands; and cruised by Jan Mayen Island on our way to Svalbard. I discovered the North Atlantic is an unforgiving place. I was sick for days.

From Jan Mayen we headed north and spent another two days at sea before pulling into Bergerbukta at the southern tip of Spitsbergen. The next four days we spent traveling the coast and fjords of the island.

The Svalbard archipelago was not what I expected. I thought it would be flatter, but it was almost all mountains and fjords. It was difficult to hike around on land because not only was it steep, but it was also covered in about two feet of snow.

We were the only people we ever saw. It was empty, cold, and kind of eerie. But the sight of the white mountains against the blue sea and sky was magical. Snow and ice, ice and water. And grey mist lingering. And when the sun finally did come out, it was beyond belief.

We saw glaciers and hiked over deep snow in Ny-London to an old deserted mining town and passed by an old blubber-gathering and whaling station.

At one point when we were headed to the northern edge of Svalbard, we came across some beautiful blue glacial ice. On the fourth day we reached 80° north. We were closer to the North Pole than to the Arctic Circle, 600 nautical miles from the North Pole and 807 nautical miles from the Arctic Circle.

On that trip I decided ships were not for me—at least ones that sailed the North Atlantic. I did not enjoy being tossed about like that. It was an experience I am glad I had, but never again.

EASTER ISLAND 2024

After having been to the southernmost city in the world and the northernmost city in the world, it was time to go west. Easter Island, otherwise known as Rapa Nui, is a five-hour flight west of Santiago, Chile. It is part of Chile and everybody there speaks Spanish.

As we approached the island I was amazed that anybody could find this little speck in the middle of the ocean. It was about the size of two Manhattan Islands. And the runway went from the ocean to the ocean, so I was glad the brakes worked. There was one flight in and one flight out to and from Santiago each day.

Today there are about 8,000 people living on Rapa Nui and about 60% are native. They are Polynesian and originally populated from other islands in the South Pacific. It is a remote place, the closest neighboring place is over 2,000 miles away.

Rapa Nui is known for its moai, large head statues sticking out of the ground. There are over 1,000 of them on the island. There was a large archeological effort in the 1980s to excavate and restore them. Those are the ones seen today. There are also many moai in museums around the world thanks to the usual looting—the British Museum, the Smithsonian, and various others. Two of the statues have been repatriated. Even today, nobody is sure how these large carvings were moved around the island or why they were made.

Rano Kau is a large extinct volcano at the southern edge of the island that is three million years old. Today there is a big lake inside it with various fruits growing around it. The island is tropical but has very few trees, since most were cut down long ago.

After we landed back in Chile, one of the people in our group showed me a photo she had taken out of the plane window. It looked like the wing had been duct-taped together. I was very glad I did not have a window seat on that trip.

PATAGONIA 2024

In southern Chile one thing I noticed while driving through the countryside from Punta Arenas to El Calafate, was just how vast and how empty it was. My sense of space became warped and my brain had a hard time processing distances. I would look out the window and it felt like I could touch the clouds or reach out and pet the animals, but they were miles away. It became more obvious when I tried to take a picture. My camera could only see a speck no matter how much I enlarged it. There were no billboards or houses, just fences and a few animals from time to time. Otherwise, about 450 miles of open space.

We spent a couple of days in Torres del Paine National Park and then we drove on to Cerro Castillo on the Chile/Argentina border. That took us all morning. Across the border we picked up National Highway 40 that runs from the Bolivian border to the southern tip of Argentina. It was 200 miles from Cerro Castillo to El Calafate and there was one town between the two. Its name was Esperanza (which means hope). The road was pretty good. We were glad to be on paved roads after the bumpy dirt roads of Torres del Paine. We arrived in El Calafate late in the afternoon.

El Calafate is on the shore of Lake Argentino, the largest freshwater lake in Argentina at 546 square miles. It is within the Glaciers National Park and its water flows to the Atlantic Ocean via the Santa Cruz River. The town has about 6,500 residents and caters to tourists with its many artsy shops, restaurants, and bars. It is also home to the Glaciarium Museum dedicated to educating people about ice and glaciers. It has an Ice Bar in it where they serve cold drinks. It is said to be the only bar in the world constructed from glacial ice.

The main attraction, of course, was Glaciers National Park and the Perito Moreno Glacier. This glacier is special because it is the only one in the world that is easily accessible to humans. It is easy to get to and to get close to. Is that good or bad? I'm not sure, but it was something to see.

This trip was also like the Egypt trip with lots of planes, eight flights total. Way too many for my comfort. I am definitely a land person. I will happily ride in a car or a bus for hours and hours. Take me anywhere, but the fewer planes the better.

ABOUT THE AUTHOR

Kathleen was born in Asia to US Expat parents. She has lived in twenty-two cities on five continents and traveled to over forty-five countries. She currently lives in Minnesota where she paints, draws, reads all the latest books on third culture kids, takes photographs, blogs from time to time, walks in the woods and tries to cook exotic meals that never seem to turn out. Oh, and she writes. Her stories have been floating around the Internet since 2011. You can find her at:

https://expatalien.blog/.

www.ingramcontent.com/pod-product-compliance
Lightning Source LLC
Chambersburg PA
CBHW032151080426
42735CB00008B/664